D1563522

SRTD
STUDIES IN RELIGION, THEOLOGY, AND DISABILITY

SERIES EDITORS

Sarah J. Melcher
Xavier University, Cincinnati, Ohio

John Swinton
University of Aberdeen, Aberdeen, Scotland

Amos Yong
Fuller Theological Seminary, Pasadena, California

Prophetic Disability

*Divine Sovereignty and Human
Bodies in the Hebrew Bible*

Sarah J. Melcher

BAYLOR UNIVERSITY PRESS

Cover Design by Kasey McBeath
Cover image: aerial view of Skeiðarárjökull, Iceland, courtesy of Unsplash/ US Geological Survey
Book Design by Baylor University Press

Hardback ISBN: 978-1-4813-1024-6
Library of Congress Control Number: 2022940198

In memory of Nancy Eiesland and Hector Avalos.
In gratitude for their friendship
and for teaching me about disability.

Series Introduction

Studies in Religion, Theology, and Disability brings newly established and emerging scholars together to explore issues at the intersection of religion, theology, and disability. The series editors encourage theoretical engagement with secular disability studies while supporting the reexamination of established religious doctrine and practice. The series fosters research that takes account of the voices of people with disabilities and the voices of their family and friends.

The volumes in the series address issues and concerns of the global religious studies/theological studies academy. Authors come from a variety of religious traditions with diverse perspectives to reflect on the intersection of the study of religion/theology and the human experience of disability. This series is intentional about seeking out and publishing books that engage with disability in dialogue with Jewish, Christian, Buddhist, or other religious and philosophical perspectives.

Themes explored include religious life, ethics, doctrine, proclamation, liturgical practices, physical space, spirituality, and the interpretation of sacred texts through the lens of disability. Authors in the series are aware of conversation in the field of disability studies and bring that discussion to bear methodologically and theoretically in their analyses at the intersection of religion and disability.

Studies in Religion, Theology, and Disability reflects the following developments in the field: First, the emergence of disability studies as an interdisciplinary endeavor that has impacted theological studies, broadly defined. More and more scholars are deploying disability perspectives in their work, and this applies also to those working in the theological academy. Second, there is a growing need for critical reflection on disability in world religions. While books from a Christian standpoint have dominated the discussion at the interface of religion and disability so far, Jewish, Muslim, Buddhist, and Hindu scholars, among those from other religious traditions, have begun to resource their own religious traditions to rethink disability in the twenty-first century. Third, passage of the Americans with Disabilities Act in the United States has raised the consciousness of the general public about the importance of critical reflection on disability in religious communities. General and intelligent lay readers are looking for scholarly discussions of religion and disability as these bring together and address two of the most important existential aspects of human lives. Fourth, the work of activists in the disability rights movement has mandated fresh critical reflection by religious practitioners and theologians. Persons with disabilities remain the group most disaffected from religious organizations. Fifth, government representatives in several countries have prioritized the greater social inclusion of persons with disabilities. Disability policy often proceeds based on core cultural and worldview assumptions that are religiously informed. Work at the interface of religion and disability thus could have much broader purchase—that is, in social, economic, political, and legal domains.

Under the general topic of thoughtful reflection on the religious understanding of disability, Studies in Religion, Theology, and Disability includes shorter, crisply argued volumes that articulate a bold vision within a field; longer scholarly monographs, more fully developed and meticulously documented, with the same goal of engaging wider conversations; textbooks that provide a state of the discussion at this intersection and chart constructive ways forward; and select edited volumes that achieve one or more of the preceding goals.

Contents

Introduction

Disability and Divine Sovereignty in the Hebrew Prophets

WHY THIS STUDY

This study constitutes the first book-length exploration of disability in the Hebrew Prophets. The specific books that will be analyzed are Isaiah, Jeremiah, Ezekiel, and the Twelve (Hosea, Joel, Amos, Obadiah, Jonah, Micah, Nahum, Habakkuk, Zephaniah, Haggai, Zechariah, and Malachi). Daniel will not be included in this study since it is found in the Writings in Jewish editions of the Tanakh. Comprehensive studies of disability in biblical literature are important at this time since biblical scholars are still learning how metaphors of disability function in these literary contexts.

METHOD AND PHILOSOPHY OF STUDY

Some recent scholarship in disability studies takes a critical realist approach that I find appealing. Tom Shakespeare devotes a chapter to describing "critical realist approaches to disability" in his book, *Disability Rights and Wrongs Revisited* (Shakespeare 2014). He states, "I am unashamedly eclectic and pragmatic in my theoretical allegiances, finding a plurality of approaches beneficial in the analysis of disability" (Shakespeare 2014, 72).

According to Shakespeare, one of the advantages of the critical realist perspective is that it allows for complexity. The theory accepts an external reality, that bodies have an independent existence apart from what people think about them. As he states, "Critical realists distinguish between ontology (what exists) and epistemology (our ideas about what exists)" (Shakespeare 2014, 73). Material things have an existence independent from what they are called. Quite sensibly, Shakespeare maintains that labels describe, they do not "constitute disease" (Shakespeare 2014, 73). In other words, impairment is a reality that has always been and there is a distinct experience associated with impairment. The critical realist approach does not resort to relativism nor to extreme constructivism. Yet, at the same time, the theory is culturally sensitive and acknowledges historical particularities.

Simon J. Williams promotes critical realism as an approach to the study of disability, because critical realism "enables us to: (i) bring the biological body, impaired or otherwise, 'back in'; (ii) relate the individual to society in a challenging, non-conflationary or non 'unidirectional' way; and (iii) rethink questions of identity, difference and the ethics of care through a commitment to real bodies and real selves, real lives and real worlds" (Williams 1999, 812–13). Critical realists, says Williams, offer an ontological defense of the body as a pre-discursive thing. They also ask how this physical, real body relates to society and how we understand disability within the context of this relationship. Williams mentions three basic ontological premises which provide a foundation for critical realism, namely *intransitivity, transfactuality*, and *stratification*. First, intransitive entities exist independently of their identification. In other words, there are intransitive objects that exist and act independently of knowledge. There are limits placed upon how we can construe an actual entity.

What is meant by the *transfactuality of mechanisms* is that at least some things are "necessary and at least relatively enduring" (Williams 1999, 808). The word "relatively" is crucial here. The critical realism model recognizes that nothing in the social world is immutable. By assuming that some things are necessary and at least relatively enduring, critical realism avoids the accusation of over-determinism, "in which structures can never be changed and social agents are stripped of social agency" (Williams 1999, 808). Critical realism also insists that reality is stratified, that analysis must look at deep structures and not rely simply on surface information. As Williams points out, the model takes into consideration temporality or vertical influences (historical particularism taken into consideration) as well as horizontal causes, those at a specific, contemporaneous time frame (Williams 1999, 808). In this approach, there is room for critical analysis of how societal structure and agency shape and reshape one another over time. This method allows for full consideration of human agency that has a critical reflexivity and creativity toward the world. The recognition of complex interactions is helpful indeed to the study of disability, because it avoids the consideration of society as being fully determinative of outcomes in favor of a more open, variable model.

Williams raises the importance of critical realism for the study of disability: "Disability, from this perspective, is an *emergent* property, located, temporally speaking, in terms of the *interplay* between the biological reality of *physiological impairment*, *structural conditioning* (i.e., *enablements/constraints*), and *socio-cultural interaction/ elaboration*" (Williams 1999, 810; emphasis original). Thus, critical realism does a fine job of dealing with disability's complexity. The model also allows for people to initiate changes in structures, which is important in disability studies.

Nick Watson offers an overview of recent work in disability studies and after his survey, concludes by recommending critical realism as an effective approach for disability studies (Watson 2012). Though he values previous research, he prefers critical realism as a method because "in critical realism, social science research is concerned with exploring how agency is influenced by structures and vice versa, without overemphasizing either agency or structure" (Watson 2012, 102). According to Watson, critical realism maintains that it is not reality itself that is socially constructed. Rather it is our theories of what is real that are constructed (Watson 2012, 102). Critical realism allows for the analysis of impairment and the daily experiences of people who have impairments. "By focusing on both structural barriers to inclusion and individual agency, critical realism allows for an approach that gives appropriate weight to the different dimensions of the disability experience" (Watson 2012, 102). Another advantage of the critical realism approach is that it can employ various methodologies, both quantitative and qualitative. It avoids the reductionism that is sometimes a problem with the social model and also successfully avoids the individualism of traditional medical sociology.

Watson discusses the contributions of a stratified or laminated system, developed by Bhaskar and Danermark (Bhaskar 2006). According to these authors, critical realism is less restrictive, allowing determinations to be made empirically on a case-by-case basis (Bhaskar 2006, 280). As Bhaskar and Danermark perceive it, "critical realism indicates more clearly than the other positions the appropriate *direction* and context of *explanatory research*—from the manifest phenomena to the mechanisms that produce them, in their complex co-determination" (Bhaskar 2006, 280; emphasis in original). Critical realism avoids the particularity of some methods, that is, the exclusive focus on one aspect of the research. As a method it accepts a vision of a laminated or multi-layered reality, in all its complexity.

Bhaskar and Danermark argue that the previous models for disability research are somewhat reductionist. They write specifically about the medical model, the socioeconomic model, and the cultural model. In practice, the medical model focused on biological or neurological mechanisms in the individual with an impairment. The socioeconomic model focused on disability as a product of barriers in the environment. In the cultural model, research focused on how disability was constructed in various cultures. According to Bhaskar and Danermark, the difficulty with the previous models is that

> each of these models accentuates just one of what are in fact a multiplicity of mechanisms involved in the formation and reproduction of disabilities. Thus individual essentialism highlights the biological; contextual essentialism, the social (or more especially the socio-economic); and social constructionism, the socio-cultural mechanisms or causal determinations. But clearly all three types of determination may play a role in the onset or maintenance of a particular disability. Of course, it is important to say, that it was not the case that these perspectives totally ignored mechanisms at other levels, but rather that there was a clear tendency in each of them to *a priori* privilege, prioritize or emphasize one type of explanatory mechanism to the detriment, often tantamount to exclusion, of the others. (Bhaskar 2006, 281; emphasis in original)

With critical realism, multiple methods and resources may be used to advantage in the study of disability. Though critical realism establishes a higher bar for the researcher, that is, she or he must take more levels and factors into consideration, there is a larger likelihood that critical realism avoids reductionism to a greater extent than some of these other approaches.

The authors suggest what a laminated (multi-leveled) system might look like. The researcher would look at "(i) physical, (ii) biological, and more specifically physiological, medical or clinical, (iii) psychological, (iv) psycho-social, (v) socio-economic, (vi) cultural and (vi) normative kinds of mechanisms, types of context and characteristic effects are all essential to the understanding of the phenomena in fields such as disability research" (Bhaskar 2006, 288–89). The authors explain the approach further by indicating that each of layers iii–vii, the social levels

> may be set in the context of the concept of four-planar social being. . . . On this concept every social event can be understood in terms of four dimensions, namely: (i) material transactions with nature; (ii) social interactions between agents; (iii) social structure proper; and (iv) the stratification of embodied personalities of agents. (Bhaskar 2006, 289)

As Shakespeare acknowledges, "The experience of a disabled person results from the relationship between factors intrinsic to the individual, and extrinsic factors arising from the wider context in which she finds herself" (Shakespeare 2014, 74–75). Contextual factors may influence the intrinsic factors; for instance, impairment may be caused by poverty or war; the individual's response to impairment may be influenced by cultural factors, etc. However, the difficulties associated with disability cannot be eliminated by making adjustments to social arrangements. Disability is a result of the interplay between impairment and context/environment. Shakespeare argues that a relational approach to disability was needed, because "disability is a relationship between intrinsic factors (impairment, personality, motivation, etc.) and extrinsic factors (environments, support systems, oppression, etc.)" (Shakespeare 2014, 76).

Of course, any analysis of the Hebrew prophets will be incapable of achieving the kind of in-depth study of disability as that envisioned using critical realism. The type of analysis represented in critical realism can examine disability in all its complexities, with all the tools of research at the ready. In the study of the Hebrew Bible, our grasp of the historical, sociological, and cultural background is necessarily limited, due to the distances of time, culture, and geography. We are also limited as to what our primary source of information is—the biblical text itself. Nevertheless, critical realism offers a model that is worthy of imitation. To the point that it is possible with an ancient text, this book will attempt to look at multiple aspects of disability and the interrelatedness of the aspects, being attentive to historical, sociological, and cultural contexts. Attention will be paid to rhetorical matters as well, since rhetoric looks at how discourse intends to persuade and to shape an attitude/response on the part of the reader/hearer.

Among the perspectives that Shakespeare presents is his position that normative ethics must be a part of the critical realist approach and he appeals to both Aristotelian ethics and the capabilities approach of Amartya Sen (Sen 1992) and Martha C. Nussbaum (Nussbaum 2006). Nussbaum has developed ten central human capabilities, "minimum core social entitlements," what each citizen should have to reach a certain predetermined level (Nussbaum 2006, 75). There may be other values that prove to be important to a person's quality of life, but the following represents Nussbaum's list at the time when *Frontiers of Justice* was published: (a) the ability to live one's life to its natural conclusion, with a reasonable quality of life; (b) good physical health, including reproductive health, sufficient nourishment, and acceptable shelter; (c) bodily integrity, that is, being able to move about freely, without violent assault, with opportunities for sexual satisfaction and choice in matters of reproduction; (d) to use one's senses, to think and reason imaginatively, and to produce creative works; (e) being able to feel and express emotions, such as love, and to form attachments; (f) to be able to form a conception of the good and to use that conception to make plans for one's life; (g) to affiliate with others and to show compassion and respect for others, as well as be treated with respect oneself; (h) to have concern and respect for and to relate to other species; (i) to play and to enjoy recreational activities; and (j) to exercise control over one's environment, politically and materially.

Nussbaum critiques some modern conceptions of the social contract for their failure to "to deal adequately with the needs of citizens with impairments and disabilities" (Nussbaum 2006, 98). She further argues that "a satisfactory account of human justice requires recognizing the equal citizenship of people with impairments, including mental impairments, and appropriately supporting the labor of caring for them and educating them, in such a way as to address the associated disabilities" (Nussbaum 2006, 98–99).

This book has been influenced both methodologically and philosophically by these theories about disability, but this study will seek to apply these specifically to the prophetic books of the Hebrew Bible, with the exception of the book of Daniel. Since Daniel is included in the Writings in Jewish editions of the Tanakh, it will not be included in this study. This book will pursue a multi-faceted approach to the study, yet the book will concentrate on the themes of disability as well as God's sovereignty and providence. The aspect of God's sovereignty and providence is of interest because there seems to be a relationship between God's sovereignty/providence and disability.

It is also true that there has never been a book-length comprehensive study on disability in the Hebrew prophets: Isaiah, Jeremiah, Ezekiel, and the Book of the Twelve (Hosea, Joel, Amos, Obadiah, Jonah, Micah, Nahum, Habakkuk, Zephaniah, Haggai, Zechariah, Malachi). Of course, there have been some important precursors to the present study. In her important book, *Biblical Corpora: Representations of Disability in Hebrew Biblical Literature*, Rebecca Raphael devotes some space to disability in Isaiah and to a brief excursus on some other prophetic books (Raphael 2008). Her analysis is focused in particular on how images of disability are used to represent different modes of divine/human communication (Raphael 2008, 119). She states,

> Given this rich and varied use of language referring to disability, an over-emphasis on the question of healing fails to grasp how deeply these images structure the prophetic mediation between God and humanity. Metaphorical or not, disability's representational role has ramifications beyond reference to people with various impairments. (Raphael 2008, 119)

The current study engages in in-depth, explicit exegesis of given passages in the prophetic books as they are encountered in the biblical text. In addition, this present study will explore how disability is related to God's sovereignty/providence. Certainly, Raphael's essay will be a conversation partner when analyzing the book of Jeremiah.

Saul M. Olyan devotes a section of his book, *Disability in the Hebrew Bible: Interpreting Mental and Physical Differences*, to "Disability in the Prophetic Utopian Vision" (Olyan 2008, 78–92). Olyan makes the observation that "when disabled persons are mentioned in these visions of an ideal future, they function, to a large degree, as vehicles for the display of Yhwh's agency . . ." (Olyan 2008, 79). Certainly, Olyan's insight is helpful here, and his book will be a conversation partner, but the present study will go into more depth at the intersection of disability and God's sovereignty/providence. Olyan's previous work does suggest the fruitfulness of exploring these relationships more deeply. His focus is on utopian prophetic visions while this study will analyze other, nonutopian prophetic texts.

Another important precursor to this study is J. Blake Couey's chapter-length work, "Isaiah, Jeremiah, Ezekiel, Daniel, and the Twelve," which examines disability in the prophetic books (Couey 2017). The chapter is carefully researched and examines many pertinent passages in the style of a biblical commentary. The author explicitly mentions that the "chapter offers close readings of prophetic texts that contain language or images associated with disability, with special attention to the relationship between disability and divine power" (Couey 2017, 216). Couey's chapter encourages further research in this area. The present study, because it will explore the prophetic biblical literature in greater depth in a book-length study, will build on Couey's work, but develop it further. This book will also apply a specific methodology, adapted from the "critical realism" approach in disability studies. As far as I know, this method has not been applied in the study of disability in the Bible. The two facets of disability and the sovereignty/providence of God and their interrelationship have not yet been used together in a book about the Hebrew prophets.

Chapter 1 will explore disability and God's sovereignty in Isaiah. Chapter 2 will explore those two facets in Jeremiah. In chapter 3 the focus will be on Ezekiel; in chapter 4, the focus will be on the Book of the Twelve; the conclusion will examine the broad theological and ethical implications of the study. Chapters 1–4 will engage in a relevant exegetical survey, while some theological implications will be incorporated briefly as relevant. The conclusion will offer a broader view of the theological and ethical implications and in more depth at the same time.

In each of these chapters, I will be attentive to several facets of a disability approach to prophetic texts, approximating a critical realist approach to the Hebrew prophets. In doing so, within the limitations noted above, I will be attentive to historical, sociological, cultural backgrounds influencing these texts as well as rhetorical means of persuading and shaping responses in readers. In addition, this study will explore disability concerns as they interrelate with portrayals of God's sovereignty/providence. The discussion of God's sovereignty/ providence is of importance to any reading of the prophetic books because the prophets are preoccupied with God's supreme power and controlling influence over the nations. These texts also are concerned with God's related care, guidance, and sustaining power for the people. God's sovereignty and power are often portrayed in relationship to themes or metaphors of disability. The interrelationship of themes of disability and God's sovereignty/providence will be revealing of social structures and mores influencing these passages.

Among the facets bearing on disability that this book will explore is the issue of physical defilement and proper worship; Yhwh's acts of physical punishment for disobedience and sinfulness; Yhwh's ability to strengthen or weaken the nations; and Yhwh's intention to include people with disabilities in the full restoration of the nation. Ethical and theological issues rise to our attention throughout the book and the concluding chapter will expand on these, keeping in mind Nussbaum's values for quality of life. The multifaceted approach to the study of disability and divine sovereignty provides a fuller picture of the treatment of disability in the prophetic literature.

1

"The Hands of All Will Go Limp"

The Book of Isaiah

As J. Blake Couey has pointed out, "Isaiah contains more references to disability than any other book in the prophetic corpus, and the imagery of blindness and deafness features especially prominently in its discourse about the divine-human relationship" (Couey 2017, 219). The present chapter will analyze two primary themes in the book of Isaiah: (a) perspectives about disability, and (b) presentations of divine sovereignty/providence. In the concluding section of this chapter, we will explore the interrelationship of these two themes. We will also consider some of the theological implications of this study.

This chapter begins with an exegetical survey of the passages that are relevant in some way to the two themes outlined above. As noted in the introduction to this book, this study will draw from multiple approaches to explore disability and divine sovereignty/providence in Isaiah.

Biblical scholars have long noted the literary and historical complexities in the formation of the book of Isaiah. Many books, articles, and essays have been devoted to the topic of the formation of the Book, for example, some of the essays in *New Visions of Isaiah*, edited by Roy F. Melugin and Marvin A. Sweeney (Melugin and Sweeney 1996). Because I have chosen to use a method that is interdisciplinary and multifaceted, I will pay some attention to the formation of the book of Isaiah in order to offer some insights of historical and sociological context for a given passage, but I hope not to go too far afield from my main task of analyzing the themes of disability and divine sovereignty in the book of Isaiah, as well as the interrelationship of these themes. There is some advantage, however, in being aware of the relationship of a given passage with other passages in the book (a synchronic approach) and the historical nuances leaving a trace in the given passage. I find the discussion of Rolf Rendtorff on various approaches to the question of formation to be helpful here (Rendtorff 1996).

FIRST ISAIAH: CHAPTERS 1–39

Isaiah 1–12: Introduction and Early Oracles

Isaiah has numerous references or allusions to disability, beginning with chapter 1. Though J. J. M. Roberts argues that verses 2–20 form a single literary unit in the present context (Roberts 2015, 18), many scholars now see the entire first chapter as serving as introduction to the book of Isaiah, especially given the superscriptions in 1:1 and 2:1 (Couey 2015, 192–93; Blenkinsopp 2000). John Goldingay argues persuasively that verses 1:1 and 2:1 serve as a framework for the entire chapter 1 which in turn serves as an introduction to some form of Isaiah 1–39 (Goldingay 1998). After the superscription in 1:1 describing Isaiah's historical context, in reference to the kings who had reigned during his career (Uzziah, Jotham, Ahaz, and Hezekiah), the voice of Yʜᴡʜ begins with familial language to confront the reader with her/his violation of the covenant. The exhortation to heaven and earth to listen to God's disputation in verse 2 may constitute a reminder to covenantal witnesses to be attentive to an accusation of covenantal violation (Roberts 2015, 20). God reminds readers that the people of Israel were raised as Yʜᴡʜ's children. This metaphoric relationship of God/Parent to Israel/Child occurs frequently in prophetic literature, including in the book of Isaiah. That Israel/Child has rebelled against God/Parent evokes covenantal language as well, since covenant violation is often construed in terms of "rebellion" as political terminology (Roberts 2015, 20). That the rebellion is against God is expressed clearly in the expression, פשעו בי ("they have rebelled against me").

Verse 3 compares Judah unfavorably to an ox or donkey. These animals recognize their master's sovereignty over them, but Judah does not. Judah's inhabitants are corrupt children who have turned away from Yhwh and abandoned their God.

Verses 5–6 liken Judah's political situation to being thoroughly wounded and ill. Most standard translations ask some version of the rhetorical question, "Why do you seek further beatings?" (NRSV; cf. JPS, NIV, etc.). A more literal translation of the phrase, taking into consideration the passive verb form תֻּכּוּ, would be, "Why be beaten any further?" Thus, at least metaphorically, Israel's afflicted state is the result of a beating. The outcome of the beating is that "every head is sick and every heart is faint" (v. 5b). Verse 6 extends the metaphor by indicating that sores and wounds cover the entire body from the sole of the foot up to the head. The community of Israel is utterly corrupt, without exception. Rebecca Raphael argues that these verses use "a metaphor of the wounded body to signify the state of a corporate entity, Judah" (Raphael 2008, 24).

Given the preceding verses, this chapter is describing the rebellion of Israel by using metaphors of violence and of illness. According to J. Blake Couey, "When cities or nations are given metaphorical bodies—an ancient variation on the idea of the 'body politic'—they are almost invariably wounded (Isa 1:5–6; Jer 14:17; 30:12–13; Hos 5:13; Nah 3:19)" (Couey 2017, 217). The body has been subjected to so many wounds and marks of beating that it is completely covered. The imagery, as noted by another scholar, is stunning (Raphael 2008, 121). This image of the body politic makes Judah's estrangement from God extensive and complete. It is an image that captures the reader's attention, but it is also an image that equates the wounded body with unfaithfulness.

Some scholars suggest that this first chapter in Isaiah was composed and redacted in order to serve as an introduction to the whole First Isaiah, 1–39 or at least to chapters 1–33. If it has been written as an introduction to the book as a whole, then the date for the introduction itself would be dated to sometime after 701, since verses 7–9 strongly suggest the military devastation caused by Sennacherib's campaign, although Niditch argues that some verses in chapter 1 reflect a postexilic theology (Niditch 1980, 528). Verses 7–9 describe Judah as desolate and its cities as consumed by fire, but Jerusalem will stand. Foreigners are presented as responsible for the devastation of the land, a portrayal that can reflect knowledge of a military siege. Whether this is an indication of the

Sennacherib campaign in Judah or it reflects a later campaign by the Babylonians is not clear. There are some similarities between verses 28–31 with 66:24 with the theme of consuming fire in each, which may suggest a postexilic date for the final form of chapter 1.

Elsewhere in the first chapter (vv. 16–18), the prophet exhorts the people to cleanse themselves and to enact justice for the widow and the orphan. If the people do not restore justice in the land, God will do the cleansing and the restoration through harsher means. One of the titles used for God in Isaiah 1 is "the Holy One of Israel" (v. 4), which brings in the relationship between holiness and uncleanness (Raphael 2008, 135). One element that emphasizes the sovereignty of God, is the aspect of God's holiness. At its root, holiness means being separated for a specific purpose. God's holiness is also related to issues of purity and impurity, as it is generally understood that one must be sanctified and pure in order to approach holiness. As Raphael states, "Isa 1:4–6 places the title Holy One of Israel into contiguity with the body composed entirely of wounds" (Raphael 2008, 135). In Isaiah 1, the Holy One of Israel intends to cleanse the people of the land. The concept of God's sovereignty is developed by statements such as, "But if you refuse and rebel, you shall be devoured by the sword; the mouth of Yнwн has spoken" (v. 20). The speech of God guarantees results, according to Isaiah. Yet, overall, the concept of God's holiness tends to create separation between God and God's people, though the people's cleansing by God may help bridge the gap.

Chapter 2, verse 3 envisions the nations streaming to the house of Yнwн in order that God "will teach us of his ways and we shall walk in his paths." The terms מדרכיו ("of his ways") and בארחתיו ("in his paths") are metaphors that are rooted in physical environs. With the addition of the verb ונלכה ("and we shall walk"), the physical basis for the metaphor is made clearer. The metaphor connotes those who adhere to God's will. Yet, at the root of the metaphor, the composer(s) of the passage envisions the nations in physical terms, as walking in the paths that God had provided. The metaphor appeals to those who do not have mobility impairments. A similar kind of metaphor appears in verse 5 where the people say, "O house of Jacob, come let us walk by the light of Yнwн." Here, again, we find the use of the verb, ונלכה ("let us walk"), used as a metaphor rooted in the physical environs.

Another important consideration in Isaiah 2 is its representation of the sovereign power of Yhwh. As Saul M. Olyan points out about the transformations reflected in the utopian visions of 2:1–4 and 11:1–9, "All of these changes are emblematic of Yhwh's incomparable power: nothing whatever is too much for him according to these texts" (Olyan 2008, 81). In chapter 2, the nations shall stream to an exalted Mount Zion to learn about God, weapons of war shall become agricultural implements, and there shall be peace among the nations. God is indeed sovereign over all, according to Isaiah 2.

The use of bodily metaphors continues in 3:8, where the prophet states, "Ah, Jerusalem has stumbled and Judah has fallen." Couey notes that this stumbling and falling may be a result of the removal of staff and stay in verse 1, referring to the removal of Judah's leadership (Couey 2017, 220–21). This metaphor depicts the city and kingdom as impacted by mobility problems and falling upon the ground. Again, Judah's political issues are portrayed in physical terms, that the kingdom is unable to stay upright. This equates military defeat with a physical image of lying on the ground. This tends to picture someone with a physical disability as defeated. The reason for Judah's fall is given later in verse 8, "Because by speech and deeds they insult Yhwh, defying the eyes of his glory." Judah's deeds and speech, what they do physically, have offended God and they have done these things in God's presence (Roberts 2015, 56). Later, in verse 11, the wicked one is threatened with a bad outcome for what "his hands have done." Verse 12 takes exception to leaders who mislead, for "they have confused the course of your paths" (דרך ארחתיך). As in 2:3, 3:12 uses metaphors that convey the concept of walking in paths. The corruption of leaders is depicted in terms of guiding people down wrong paths. Thus, the corruption of Judah's leaders is portrayed in terms of physical mobility, moving in appropriate ways down appropriate paths.

Another strategy of the composer(s) of chapter 3 is to suggest that the people of Judah have become arrogant and feminine imagery is used to communicate that. Verses 16–26 describe the nation of Judah as haughty women who stretch their necks high in their arrogance, gaze wantonly at others, and tinkle when they walk (presumably because they are wearing jewels or bells on their ankles). The text indicates at length what God will do to those women mentioned in verse 16. In fact, God's actions to humble the women are enumerated in ten verses compared to the one verse depicting the women's offenses. God will give the women scabs on the crowns of their heads and uncover their foreheads. An extensive list is given of the various items that mark the women as wealthy and haughty: anklets, bracelets, earrings, shawls, scarves, etc. Even their husbands will be killed in battle, then the women will be reduced to lament and to sitting on the ground. As J. J. M. Roberts states, "The transformation of perfume to stench, elaborate hairdos to baldness, riches to rags—all of these simply illustrate how Yahweh will turn these women's beauty into their shame" (Roberts 2015, 65). The women are depicted as humiliated as representatives of the disobedience of Judah, the people's failure to live faithfully before God. Both people with disabilities and women are used metaphorically to illustrate Judah's distance from God.

Isaiah 4:1 continues with the humiliation of the women of Judah by portraying seven of them begging one man "to take away our reproach" by giving them a name, though the women agree to provide for their own apparel and food. Verse 4 renews the use of a humiliating portrayal of women to envision a time when Judah and Jerusalem have been purified. There is an allusion to rinsing menstrual blood which the reader will associate with removing ritual impurity. Other prophetic passages also use menstruation to indicate moral impurity (for example Ezekiel 22:10 and 36:17). This use of a natural process to signify moral impurity is demeaning to women. Yet, after the purification of the people, Yhwh's presence is then seen on Mt. Zion in the form of a cloud by day and smoke with flaming fire at night, which is reminiscent of the story of God's presence in the wilderness in Exodus.

Isaiah 5:26–30 represents the military forces of Assyria as tireless, without need of sleep, and the troops do not stumble. Their capabilities as soldiers are compared to lions and they seize their prey in a similar way. In order to emphasize the effectiveness of Assyria's military, the soldiers are pictured as physically strong, in fact, super strong, without suffering fatigue like most human beings. To portray some human beings as beyond human weakness is not a favorable depiction for people with disabilities. No soldiers are so effective that they do not tire, and it is a potentially harmful representation.

The prophetic commissioning passage of Isaiah 6:1–13 famously employs bodily metaphors to indicate moral failure. In verse 5, Isaiah the prophet declares himself to be "a man of unclean lips" and he lives among "people of unclean lips." A seraph in attendance upon Yнwн purges impurity from Isaiah's lips with a live coal. When Isaiah responds willingly to God's call, he is given a task in terms relevant for our study (verses 9–10): "Go! And tell this people; Hear, indeed, but do not understand. See, indeed, but do not perceive. Dull the people's mind; shut its eyes; lest, seeing with its eyes and hearing with its ears, it would understand with its heart, turn and heal itself." Couey remarks that this constitutes poetic justice, since Judah's leaders' refusal to hear, see, and understand is answered by the people's inability to hear, see, and understand (Couey 2017, 222). In the words of Raphael, "the prophet's speech itself becomes disabling, the means by which these impairments are effected" (Raphael 2008, 122). As we have seen before, a feature of the body is portrayed as impure and its cleansing is seen as removing the consequences of sin. Perhaps the reference to people who will not understand or perceive is to illustrate the last-ditch effort that Isaiah's task represents (Roberts 2015, 102). According to the text, the call of Isaiah took place in the year that King Uzziah died. Roberts argues that this historical superscription would not be necessary unless it was written after the event (Roberts 2015, 91). This likely occurred in 733 BCE, at a time when Judah was clearly impacted by the Syro-Phoenician conflict. The chapter closes with the devastation of the land, a depiction in keeping with the actions of Aram and Israel against Judah.

Isaiah 10 portrays God as using the Assyrian king and his forces to punish Judah. Later, however, because of the arrogance of Assyria, God's actions punish the Assyrians. Verses 16–19, in particular, use imagery that is of interest to this project. God is portrayed as sending a "wasting sickness" among the stout ones of Assyria. This punishment is followed by a fire that will consume most of the bushes. There is a consistency in imagery; the idea that all things would be consumed through God's actions. Heavy people would be consumed by a wasting sickness that was brought through God's initiative. It is problematic that God is depicted as causing serious illness among the people of Assyria. Yet, as Joseph Blenkinsopp notes, the passage "illustrates an important aspect of the message of Israel's prophets, i.e., the critique of imperialism and the refusal to take nationalistic and imperialistic pretensions seriously on their own terms" (Blenkinsopp 2000, 256).

Chapter 11 deals with the advent of an ideal king and employs metaphors of the body to picture what the ideal king will be like. According to Roberts, this ideal king will be from the lineage of David but will be more like David than the current king, Ahaz (Roberts 2015, 179). For the ideal king will have the spirit of YHWH upon him, a spirit which conveys wisdom, discernment, counsel, and strength (v. 2). Verse 3 indicates specifically that the new king shall not make decisions based upon what he sees or hears. This king, apparently, will give careful thought to his decisions, but not through his senses of seeing and hearing. Indeed, he will be highly just in what he does, acting righteously for the poor and arbitrating with equity for the humble of the land. Continuing, verse 4 states, "He shall strike the earth with the rod of his mouth, and with the breath of his lips he shall kill the wicked." Though the king will not depend on his senses to make decisions, relying instead on the spirit of YHWH, he is nevertheless portrayed as a physically powerful actor. With the rod of his mouth and the breath of his lips, he will cause the death of wicked persons. Further, verse 5 indicates his apparel will make his virtues apparent, in that he will wear righteousness as a belt around his waist and "faithfulness the belt around his loins." This eschatological passage is probably later than the late eighth or early seventh centuries BCE with its very positive vision of the future. Supporting that late date, Blenkinsopp argues that some of the "distinctive vocabulary in the poem" indicate a later date (Blenkinsopp 2000, 264). The physical metaphors mentioned above extol the virtues of the future king as one who would be attentive to righteousness and justice. The consequences of the reign of this ideal king would be peace on God's holy mountain. Zion will be a safe place and knowledge of YHWH will spread throughout the land. This model king will become a symbol to the nations. This king's reign will bring exiled people back to the land of Judah, justice will *be* extant in the land, and people will live in peace. It is interesting that in some ways, Isaiah 11 downplays the role of the senses in making decisions, suggesting that the senses are not always reliable.

Chapters 13–23: Oracles against the Nations

Chapter 13, verses 6–9, uses body imagery to represent the reaction of the people of Babylon to God's actions against them. God's power will be so overwhelming that "hands of all will go limp" and "the heart of every man will melt." It is not unusual for the Hebrew Bible's writers to indicate a physical weakness or melting in response to God's efforts against a political enemy or in response to Israel's warriors when they are supported by God and close at hand. Framed as the advent of the day of YHWH in verse 9, the physical weakness is then seen as punishment attendant upon that day. Stricken with fear, the Babylonians will be in pain and agony: "They will be in anguish like a woman in labor" (v. 8a). The writers portray the Babylonians as without physical strength because of their fear and they are compared to a woman in labor because they will suffer pain when the day of YHWH comes. The portrayal of physical weakness as linked to fear can be an unfortunate association for people with disabilities in cases where weakness is manifested as a feature of the disability.

Body metaphors are persuasive in chapter 14, when the mock lament relates the fall of Israel's oppressor. Verses 24–27 portray God as ending Assyria's oppression. These verses depict God using physical power to eliminate Assyria's threat against Israel. God breaks Assyria in God's land and crushes Assyria on the holy mountain of God. As Assyria's yoke drops off of Judah, God's arm is poised to exert control over all the nations, enacting the divine plan for these peoples (Blenkinsopp 2000, 289). God is so powerful that only stretching out God's hand over the nations can change their direction to align with the divine will. To emphasize God's sovereignty over all people, the passage employs physical metaphors that illustrate God's mighty power. Assyria will be physically broken because of divine power.

A reprise of the theme of terror at the thought of YHWH punishing an enemy of Judah occurs in 19:16, but the fear that Egypt experiences makes the Egyptians like women. So, as we have seen above in 13:8a, fear of YHWH makes the Egyptians (or Babylonians) like women. Being fearful is something more typical of women or they react in a more extreme way, according to those who compiled or wrote this passage, to the denigration of women. Chapter 21, verse 3, combines the metaphors of disability and women to portray the Babylonians shrinking in fear at the prospect of God taking action against them. In response to a vision by the prophet, he describes his emotional turmoil in physical terms: "Therefore, my loins are filled with anguish. Pangs have taken hold of me like the pangs of a woman in labor; too distressed to hear and too dismayed to see" (also see 26:17–18 and Couey 2017, 223). Roberts makes the point that "the prophet reacts to this real or anticipated bad news in stereotypical fashion, with writhing and anguish like a pregnant woman in birth pangs" (Roberts 2015, 277). This association of women, especially women in labor, with fearfulness has been used repetitively and it is disparaging to women. In verse 4 the passage goes on to portray the Babylonian as having a confused, stunned mind and shuddering in panic. The prophet experiences temporary disability caused by fear (Couey 2017, 223).

Chapters 24–27

It is important to acknowledge that restoration of the people to their land and the renewal of the land is promised in chapters 24–27 of Isaiah (Stulac 2018, 105). Subsequent texts, whether they originated prior to the historical context generating chapters 24–27 or not, should be read within the canonical context of the promise of restoration. Thus, those texts of Isaiah following 24–27 in the current arrangement cannot be interpreted as indicating restoration as a surprise, since that promise was made in 24–27 (Stulac 2018, 105).

Chapters 28–35

According to 28:13, those who mock Isaiah's conveying of the word of Yhwh as simply precept after precept, and line upon line, will walk, but fall backward. Once fallen, then they are subject to be broken, snared, and taken away. Those who fail to take God's message seriously will be subject to physical defeat. Those who do not heed the word that Isaiah has transmitted will be smitten by a scourge which will beat them down (v. 18). These verses associate physical brokenness with punishment for disobedience.

Metaphors of disability figure prominently in chapter 29 of Isaiah. While verses 1–8 indicate that salvation will be grounded in the particular place of Zion (Stulac 2018, 106), verse 9 invites the listeners or readers to "stupefy yourselves and be stupefied; blind yourselves and be blind! They are drunk, but not with wine; they stagger, but not from intoxicating drink." In the following verse, metaphors of the body indicate that God has hidden reality from the prophets and seers: "Yhwh has poured upon you a spirit of deep sleep; he has closed your eyes, you prophets; and covered your heads, you seers" (v. 10). Verse 11 compares this situation to presenting someone a sealed document and commanding that they read it or presenting a similar command to someone who cannot read. Further, in verse 13, God declares that people have approached God with their mouths and honored God with their lips, but their hearts are far from God. As one reads the following verse, God promises to further baffle the people of Judah. Verses 9–14 use body metaphors to suggest that the people of Judah are not faithful and only give lip service to being devoted to God. God responds to this lack of devotion by confusing the people of Judah.

Another poem (29:15–24) uses body metaphors to remind readers of God's sovereignty. Verse 16 prompts readers to maintain a proper relationship with God: "You turn things upside down! Shall the potter be regarded as the clay? Shall the thing made say of its maker, 'He did not make me'; or the thing formed say of the one who formed it, 'He has no understanding'?" God's sovereignty is rooted in the act of creation, according to Isaiah 29. God was the one who "formed" the human being and the person "formed" should not call God's actions into question nor God's understanding. The human being's existence is entirely dependent upon God and human beings should act accordingly and not question God's choices. Daniel J. Stulac describes a general orientation of the texts in chapters 29–32, stating that "the text highlights the necessity of acknowledging one's creaturely identity before Yhwh" (Stulac 2018, 101). In the particular poem of 29:15–24, the passage "puts the difference between divinity and humanity into the highest possible relief—the Potter is sentient, animate, and creative, while the 'thing-shaped' is only 'clay' (29:16; חֹמֶר)" (Stulac 2018, 112). Verse 17 of the poem promises that Lebanon will be transformed into farmland and farmland will become forest. Verse 18 expands the transformation to include the deaf and the blind: "On that day, the deaf will hear the words of the book and out of gloom and darkness the eyes of the blind shall see." Schipper notes that verses 17–24 (and verse 18 in particular) marks one of the occasions in Isaiah where healing of people with disabilities is part of a great environmental transformation (Schipper 2015, 327–28). Verse 19 continues the transformation: "The humble will increase their joy in Yhwh and the neediest people shall exult in the holy one of Israel." While the restoration in verse 18 envisions physical cure for the deaf and the blind, the following verse through parallelism sets up an equivalence of the blind and deaf with the needy and humble (Olyan 2008, 36). This equivalence can be problematic as people with disabilities are not always needy or humble, though that is a frequent stereotype. Raphael suggests, "the appearance of humbled figures later in the chapter may well be an extension of these images. In that case, the language of disability extends to the restored state of the powerful audience that was attacked, disabled, and then humbled" (Raphael 2008, 126).

However, the final poem, verses 15–24, envisions a transformation in Judah's fortunes. Roberts' premise that the passage was written after Sennacherib's destructive campaign through Judah is notable (Roberts 2015, 376), though other later audiences would have seen the poem as pertinent as well. Couey maintains that both 29:18 and 35:5 are later developments, though they occur before Isaiah 40–55 in the arrangement of the book, since they depict the future healing of disabled bodies (Couey 2017, 219). Yet the memory of the devastation of Sennacherib's campaign through Judah would have lingered long after the events. In this poem, in verse 18, the poet envisions healing for the deaf and the blind: "On that day, the deaf shall hear the words of a scroll, and out of gloom and darkness, the eyes of the blind shall see." Raphael observes, "In Isa 29, several clear links between the initial and final situations suggest that the healings do not refer to actual deaf and blind persons, but rather continue the use of sensory impairment to represent right and wrong communication" (Raphael 2008, 125). In addition, the deaf and the blind are closely associated with the humble and the needy, who are promised joy through Yhwh, in whom they will exult (v. 19). The power and plan of Yhwh is demonstrated through people with disabilities in this passage, who are the objects of divine transformative power.

Chapter 30 represents the people of Judah as a rebellious people, "faithless children, children who will not hear the instruction of Yhwh" (v. 9). They are "seers who do not see; prophets who do not prophesy right things; speak to us falsehoods; prophesy delusions" (v. 10). While verses 9 and 10 portray the people of Judah as lacking the ability to see and prophesy well, verse 11 uses another common physical metaphor to picture the Judahites as promoting unfaithfulness: "Leave the way, turn aside from the path, let us hear no more about the holy one of Israel." The physical metaphor of turning aside from the path indicates a failure to follow God's way of living.

So, the physical inability to stay on a firm path suggests wandering from God's stipulated guidelines for faithful life.

Isaiah 30:20–21 take up the metaphor of walking the path again, and the verses tell the readers that their eyes will now be on their Teacher and if they deviate either to the right or the left, they will hear that Teacher telling them which road they should follow. Once again, the physical metaphor of walking on a path is used to represent individuals adhering to God's way of life. Anyone who is not able to stay on the path is depicted as not adhering to God's stipulations. Blenkinsopp suggests that "the walking metaphor for the moral conduct of life (verbal stem *hlk*) and the metaphor of the way (*derek*) for its direction, are drawn from the predominantly moralistic didacticism of the sages (e.g., Prov 1:15; Ps 1:1)" (Blenkinsopp 2000, 421). Yet, the idea of following the way of God and not turning right or left is found in Deuteronomy as well; for example, Deut 5:32: "You must therefore be careful to do as the LORD your God has commanded you; you shall not turn to the right or to the left." The same kind of expression is found in Deuteronomy 28:14: "And if you do not turn aside from any of the words that I am commanding you today, either to the right or to the left, following other gods to serve them."

In verses 27–33, a passage describing the destruction of Assyria, God is portrayed as physically super-powerful. God's wrath is terrifying indeed, as God comes in blazing wrath: "His lips are full of fury, his tongue like devouring fire" (v. 27). According to verse 28, God's breath is like an overflowing torrent, up to one's neck. God is depicted in frightening terms, but in very powerful ones, in compelling contrast to the metaphors describing the unfaithful people of Assyria. This daunting imagery occurs again in verse 30, where God's majestic voice is heard and the descending blow of the arm is seen, and God comes in devouring fire and with a cloudburst and rainstorm. God is remarkably powerful in comparison with the people who are the recipients of God's action. This contrast between God and human beings is stark and is a recurring motif in Isaiah in order to remind the reader of God's sovereignty and power.

Chapter 32 continues some of the same metaphors we have seen before in passages about restoration. The Davidic king of the restoration shall rule in righteousness and the king's ministers will decide with justice. The king and the ministers will be like a refuge or shelter for the people of Judah. Life in Judah will be wonderful in the reign of this king. In fact, the people will experience transformation related to their abilities: "Then the eyes of those who have sight shall not be closed, And the ears of those who have hearing shall listen; And the heart of the rash ones shall perceive knowledge, And the tongues of stammerers will be ready to speak plainly" (vv. 3–4). The people, when they use their abilities, will be attentive to what they see and hear and they will think and speak clearly. Verse 5 indicates that a good for nothing person will no longer be called noble, nor a knave said to be generous. The transformation will be remarkable. The people of Judah will acknowledge the presence of individuals who do ungodly deeds and who let the hungry, thirsty, and needy go without remedy (vv. 6–7).

The chapter goes on to challenge women who are living at ease and who are too complacent to listen to the voice of God (v. 8). It does not pay to be complacent, apparently, because the vineyards will fail as well as the fruit harvest (v. 9). Roberts argues that these two verses show that Isaiah "is attacking the same selfish unconcern of the ruling class for the welfare of the rest of the nation, and, curiously enough, for their own long-term well-being" (Roberts 2015, 415). Grief will come to them, as well, because of the failed harvest, and they will mourn upon their breasts (v. 12). These verses do not seem too demeaning to women, given that the passage indicates that all people of Judah will suffer setbacks. The latter part of the chapter, verses 15–20, indicates that Judah will experience restoration, beginning with a spirit from on high that will be poured out upon the people (v. 15). Accompanying the restoration will be justice, righteousness, and peace throughout the land (vv. 16–18).

The poem beginning with verse 2 of chapter 33 uses the imagery of Yhwh's arm to request God's strength be with the people of Judah. To develop the idea of God's power, verse 3 states, "before your majesty, nations scattered." In verse 5, Yhwh is exalted, and dwells on high, a statement which enhances God's authority and power. God brings justice and righteousness to Zion and provides stability for the era, along with salvation, wisdom, and knowledge. All of this prompts Judah to hold to its treasure, "reverence for Yhwh" (v. 6). The exaltation of Yhwh is emphasized again in verse 10, where God will raise the divine self. God threatens to devour the people with fire and those who live far away will acknowledge God's might. Only the righteous will withstand the onslaught of God's devouring fire, that is, the one "who stops his ears from hearing bloodshed and shuts his eyes from seeing evil" (v. 15). Metaphors of ability are used to show how the righteous individual would behave. Verse 16 assures the righteous that God will see to their protection and their nutritional needs. Yet, God makes the promise that foreigners will no longer be found in Judah: "You will no longer see the insolent people, people of speech too obscure to understand, stammering in a language that you cannot comprehend" (v. 19).

In fact, 33:17–24 paints a picture of glorious transformation through Yʜwʜ's hand. So complete will this transformation be that at that time "much spoil will be divided and even the lame will seize booty" (v. 23). The chapter ends with the claim that "no inhabitant will say, 'I am sick'" (v. 24a). God's transformation will be so complete that people with mobility disabilities will be able to share in the spoil and no one in the land will be ill. The passage uses metaphors of disability to highlight God's transformative power. People with disabilities will be included in the remnant who returns to Zion, to celebrate this victory (Schipper 2015, 324).

Chapter 35 depicts another magnificent restoration, following the prediction of Edom's disastrous calamity. As part of this remarkable renewal, verse 3 envisions a physical transformation: "Strengthen the weak hands, and make firm the feeble knees." Verse 4 continues this physical depiction: "Say to the fearful-hearted, 'be strong; do not fear'; behold, your God will come with vengeance, with terrible recompense. He will come and save you." A physical strengthening is a significant part of restoration. In verse 5, the theme of physical restoration comes to a pinnacle: "Then the eyes of the blind will be opened and the ears of the deaf will be unstopped." Verse 6 continues the theme with: "Then the lame shall leap like a deer; and the tongue of the mute shall sing with joy." The eschatological restoration will be one where those with disabilities will be cured. People with disabilities again serve as a foil to illustrate God's restorative power. In keeping with the master restoration, the people with disabilities are not simply healed of their disabilities but are gifted with abilities beyond what is ordinarily expected (Schipper 2015, 331).

The conclusion of chapter 35 repeats the theme of the path. In the eschatological future, none shall stray from the path, nor shall any ferocious animal walk upon it. The path is for the redeemed and the ransomed to return to Zion. All who are redeemed and/or ransomed shall be able to return via the path, with no impediment.

SECOND ISAIAH: CHAPTERS 40–55

According to Joseph Blenkinsopp (Blenkinsopp, *Isaiah 40–55: A New Translation with Introduction and Commentary*, 2000), Isaiah 56–66 has a continuity of interpretation with Isaiah 40–55 but not a continuity of authorship. He acknowledges that Bernhard Duhm's (Duhm 1922) division of 40–55 and 56–66 has stood firm over decades of interpretation (Blenkinsopp, *Isaiah*, 2000, 70). While Isaiah 40–55 seems to reflect a historical situation at the end of the exile, Blenkinsopp argues that 56–66 reflects a different historical background and a different agenda.

Perhaps the most significant theme of chapter 40 is the sovereignty of God. The chapter emphasizes God's power, faithfulness, and compassion, but focuses throughout on God's oversight and providential care in all things. The glory of God will be revealed (v. 5), God's word is reliable (v. 5), God's word is eternal (v. 8), God is mighty and brings reward and recompense (v. 10), and God will take care of God's flock (v. 11). God's reliability is expressed in physical terms as God's glory is revealed because "the mouth of YHWH has spoken" (v. 5). A very effective theme for stressing God's sovereignty appears in verse 12, reminding the reader of God's role in creation. As verse 12a represents it, God's incomparability is closely related to God's sovereignty: "Who has measured the waters in the hollow of his hand; and marked off the heavens with a span?" To ask these questions, the verse stresses the distinction between the divine and humanity (Balzer 2001, 67). Verses 13 and 14 emphasize God's incomparability by pointing out that God had no counselors nor advisers in the creative process. Who can do what God has done?

In contrast to God's power and incomparability, verses 6–7 of chapter 40 emphasize the fragility of human life, its fleeting nature. Perhaps the prophet refers to the Babylonians as being impermanent humanity, easily taken down by YHWH through YHWH's anointed (Blenkinsopp 2000, 183–84). The nations are diminished in the comparison with God, emphasizing God's authority over the surrounding, inconsequential nations (vv. 15–17). As Balzer points out in regard to verse 17, "this relativizes all power, not only the power of rulers. This is a matter of faith, no longer something that can be demonstrated. Fear is confronted by experience of the reality of God's power" (Balzer 2001, 71). Idols compare unfavorably with God, as portrayed in verses 18–20. Latter verses continue to stress God's power and sovereignty, contrasting the inconsequential nature of humanity; for example, in v. 22, "Its inhabitants are like grasshoppers."

Though the contrast between the power of God and the fleeting nature of life as a human are both emphasized in the ending verses of chapter 40, God also promises to strengthen human beings: "He gives power to the faint, and strengthens the powerless" (v. 29). Even the young may grow weary, but those who wait on or hope in God will renew their strength (vv. 30–31). Though the passage normalizes human weakness, God is a source of strength for those who rely upon God.

Marvin A. Sweeney states that "Isaiah 41:1–42:13 is both a formal and rhetorical unit that argues that Yhwh is the master of human events" (Sweeney 2016, 78). He suggests that the passage presupposes Cyrus' decree of 539 BCE permitting the Jews' return to the land of Israel and the rebuilding of the temple in Jerusalem (Sweeney 2016, 78). In fact, Sweeney says, "The presumption of the servant, Israel's return to the land of Israel throughout the passage appears to presuppose that Cyrus's decree has already been issued" (Sweeney 2016, 78).

The portrayal of the sovereignty of God and its relationship to disability motifs is a primary interest of this book. Chapter 41 certainly highlights God's sovereignty in lending Cyrus the power to defeat nations and their rulers. Yet, Yhwh's power over the nations is especially prominent in the divine treatment of Jacob. God assures Israel, God's servant, that the people have been chosen and will not be cast off (see vv. 8–10). These servants have been taken from the ends of the earth and called from its farthest corners. God promises to impart strength to them and to help them (v. 10).

The people of Judah were able to survive exile and return because of the power of God to rule over the various peoples of the area (see vv. 11–16). The Redeemer, the Holy One of Israel, will turn the Judean people into powerful warriors against those nations who would challenge them. They shall scatter the nations like chaff and then they shall rejoice in Yhwh and glory in God (v. 16). God's creative power will provide water for the poor and needy, opening rivers, pools, fountains, and springs in the wilderness (vv. 17–18). God will place the cedar, the myrtle, and other trees so that all will know that God has done this (vv. 19–20). To present the greatest challenge of all, God invites the gods of the other nations to prove their worth and their ability to effect change, but the gods' efforts are futile. The entire chapter illustrates God's ability to determine the shape of history.

Though Isaiah 42:1–4 refers to Yhwh's servant with third masculine Hebrew forms, if it is consistent with other servant passages (49:1–6; 50:4–11; 52:13–53:12), the servant is identified with Israel/Jacob. This will be the assumption here, as it has been for other scholars (Sweeney 2016). Israel/Jacob in the context of the late sixth century or early fifth century is represented in this passage as teaching the nations the way of Yhwh (vv. 1 and 4). The servant is especially gentle, not causing harm to others (vv. 2–3). No harm will come to the servant, either, until he establishes "the true way on earth" (v. 4).

Verse 5 reminds the reader of God's creative power and that a person's very breath is dependent upon Yhwh. In the following verse God describes the reasons for the calling of Israel to the nations: "I am Yhwh, who called you in righteousness. I have taken you by the hand and kept you; I have given you as a covenant to the people, a light to the nations" (v. 6). God's servant will live in service to the people and in service to God. Israel is tasked with opening "the eyes of the blind; to bring out prisoners from the dungeon, from the prison those who sit in darkness" (v. 7). This verse associates people who have disabilities with prisoners (Olyan 2008, 36). Couey states that "Isaiah 42:7 thus depicts the servant's role in the liberation of exiles using characteristically Isaianic language of restoring sight to blind persons" (Couey 2017, 233). Yet, as Schipper notes, the servant is not healed of disability (Schipper 2015, 325). In addition, Israel's commission, while it is primarily to lead people to God, also includes restoring sight to the blind—that is, curing people with that disability. This vision of restoration, channeled through servant Israel, removes people who have a disability from view. This portion of the chapter ends in verse 9 with a promise that God will inaugurate new things, and curing the blind is part of the new things.

In the section 42:13–17, God becomes a warrior on Israel's behalf. Verse 14 is of particular interest for our study because the passage uses the metaphor of a woman in labor to describe God's activity;

she screams, pants, and gasps. After God decimates the countryside in verse 15, the passage uses disability metaphors to depict God's help in returning the exiles to Judah: "I will lead the blind by a road they do not know; by paths they do not know I will guide them. I will make the darkness before them into light, the rough places into level ground. These are things I will do and I will not forsake them" (v. 16). Probably, the purpose of the disability metaphors is to illustrate that God will return the exiles to the land of Judah in spite of any obstacles. It suggests that God will make accommodations to make sure that everyone can return to the land. An interesting feature is the statement by God in verse 16 that through divine power, the rough places will be made level. It reminds this reader of cuts made in curbs to allow wheelchairs to pass through. The promise of continued divine presence is encouraging. Verse 17 closes this small section by contrasting the treatment of idol worshipers with those who are faithful to God.

The disability metaphors recur in verses 18–21 of chapter 42. Those who are deaf are exhorted to listen and those who are blind are urged to look up and see (v. 18). In verse 19, God asks the question of who is blind but God's servant and who is deaf like God's messenger. God is asking who is blind like Israel, who, when the exile is ended, has no idea what his/her role in God's plan might be. Later, in verse 20, God says that Israel, God's servant, sees and hears many things, but does not understand the significance of the observations and the sounds he/she is privy to. Yet, these disability metaphors depict people who needed God's help to get back to the land. They imply that the people with disabilities cannot return on their own initiative or find the means to come back on their own. The disability metaphors are also used in verses 18–20 to suggest a lack of spiritual insight among the people of Israel. Chapter 42 closes with a sympathetic view of the people and the terrible hurt that they had experienced through the exile, but the passage makes it clear that the exile occurred because God intended it as punishment for Israel's misdeeds. To illustrate Israel's faithlessness, the people are portrayed as wandering from God's ways or paths (v. 24).

Isaiah 43:5–8 envisions the deity returning the exiles to their homeland. Among those who will be gathered back to the land are the blind and the deaf. Verse 8 states, "Bring forth the people who are blind, yet have eyes, who are deaf, yet have ears!" As Jeremy

Schipper argues, the fact that the returnees have eyes that are non-functional and have ears but do not hear, demonstrates that this ingathering does not imply healing. Rather, the verse may allude to Isaiah 6:10, where the prophet is commanded to shut the peoples' eyes and stop their ears (Schipper 2015, 323).

Yнwн invites the nations to indicate when their prophets' predictions came true in verse 43:9 and bring witnesses to verify these predictions. Verses 10–13 remind the reader or listener that Yнwн is the only God and that the people of Israel are witnesses to God's predictions and their fulfillment. Other gods cannot have witnesses that testify to the truth and fulfilment of their predictions because, as verse 11 states definitively, "I, I am Yнwн and there is no savior besides me." Verse 13 states that when God acts, no one else can reverse that act. These verses establish God's sovereignty over all and God's authenticity. No one else can offer prophecies that come true and no other gods have the authentic power of Yнwн.

The great prediction of chapter 43 is summarized in verse 14: "Thus said the Lord, the Redeemer, the Holy One of Israel, 'For your sake, I send to Babylon, I will bring down all bars. And the Chaldeans shall raise their voice in lamentation.'" Verses 16–21 remind the reader that God redeemed the people from Egypt and in the exodus led them through the wilderness. Yet, God tells the people not to be stuck in the past because their sovereign will do a new thing. As God redeemed Israel in the past, God will lead the people through the wilderness as they return to Judah. Yet, the end of the chapter clarifies that God redeems Israel in spite of the sins of their ancestors, redeeming them for God's own sake (vv. 22–28).

The beginning of chapter 44 establishes God's power to redeem Israel and to comfort that nation. Because God created and formed Israel, God reassures Israel: "Fear not, for I have redeemed you; I have singled you out by name, you are mine" (v. 1b). Though Israel will face daunting physical challenges, through streams and fire, God will protect the people (v. 2). God is "the Holy One of Israel, your savior" who will exchange other nations in order to redeem Israel (vv. 3–4). Also, in verse 4, God reminds Israel that they are the recipients of divine love. In verses 5–8, God gives the promise that Israel will return from exile, "Bring forth the people who are blind, yet have eyes; who are deaf, yet have ears" (v. 8). Once again, Second Isaiah uses disability metaphors to convey an impression of a people who do not yet see their pivotal role in Yhwh's plan. As exiles who have been through streams and fire, it is small wonder that the people of Israel cannot discern their calling as God's messenger people. Yet God continues to remind Israel of their importance within the sovereign plan for the future.

The metaphor of Babylon as Queen in Isaiah 47 is germane to this study because we have been particularly interested in how the prophets use metaphors of women and people with disabilities. It is important to see how these metaphors are related to one another and how they differ. From the beginning of the chapter, Queen Babylon is depicted in reduced circumstances. She is commanded to sit in the dust without a throne (v. 1). She is treated like a slave woman and expected to grind food (v. 2). Fallen Babylon is commanded to strip to work, and then she strips as a precursor to rape (vv. 2–4; Franzmann 1995, 4). The Hebrew phrase that is translated "to uncover nakedness" is used frequently in the Hebrew Bible to signify sexual intercourse and that is its likely meaning here. The language of stripping is followed by God's stated intention of exacting vengeance. This is a demeaning metaphor, to be sure, but perhaps the most problematic issue is that Yhwh is the apparent perpetrator of rape (vv. 3–4; Franzmann 1995, 12–13). God's punishment for Babylon, after she has held the exiles from Judah captive for many years, is to rape her, at least metaphorically. This kind of language is abhorrent to a reader in modern times, but in the postexilic era, it signified a God capable of exacting vengeance (v. 3).

Certainly, it was conventional in the Hebrew Bible to speak metaphorically about cities using feminine language and imagery, so that is not out of the ordinary. Yet, in Isaiah 14 the king of Babylon is also portrayed in reduced circumstances, but there are no sexual connotations in what happens to him. The oppressor has been rendered powerless, but without rape. However, death awaits him and he will be greeted by other kings in Sheol (v. 15).

Nevertheless, in a strongly patriarchal culture, it is not surprising that Yhwh is pictured as a warrior and one who sexually abuses a woman as part of the activities of war. Yet, modern readers do not like to see God portrayed in this fashion. In addition, the rape of a woman is terribly demeaning. It is also shocking to see metaphors that denigrate people with disabilities.

Verse 6 in chapter 47 reminds Babylon that she did not show mercy to the exiles. In fact, Babylon placed heavy burdens on the elderly (also, v. 6). Thus, the vulnerable were oppressed by Babylon, a point which is pursued at length by Gregory L. Cuéllar (Cuéllar 2015). Indeed, Isaiah 47 depicts the downfall of the Babylonian empire. To portray the impression that the exiles were heavily oppressed, Isaiah 47 depicts the elderly as burdened. Taking Queen Babylon to task, the passage states: "You trusted in your wickedness; you said, 'no one sees me' . . . you thought to yourself, 'I am and there is none but me'" (v. 10). The end of the chapter warns Babylon that magic or incantations will not save her from punitive measures enacted by God. Neither her arrogance, nor her spells would keep her from God's vengeance.

Chapter 48 represents Jacob as stubborn using the imagery of a neck of an iron sinew and a brass forehead (v. 4). This illustrates the idea of Israel being obstinate to the point of having a stiff neck. Verse 8 brings up a familiar theme where the lack of knowledge of God or failure to be faithful to the divine will is described as a problem with the senses: "You did not hear and you did not know; from long ago your ear was not opened. I knew that you were treacherous and that you were called a rebel from birth" (v. 8). This repeats a common motif in which a person is depicted as religiously deficient through the use of metaphors of disability. Similar motifs appear in chapter 50, where verse 5 declares that "the Lord God has opened my ear and I was not rebellious, nor did I turn backward." Using physical metaphors, the passage communicates that Israel is listening to God's instruction and the nation is no longer rebellious.

Isaiah 51:8 reminds the reader that human life is fleeting, but that God's salvation will endure forever. Verse 9 alludes to God's creative power and the following verse suggests God's actions in parting the sea during Israel's exodus from Egypt. God's acts of power in the past make God's promise for the future believable. These verses emphasize the contrast between God and the people of Judah. God is utterly reliable and enduring, while human life is ephemeral. Verse 11 reassures the reader that the exiles redeemed by God will return to Zion through God's dependable clout.

Jeremy Schipper has done an in-depth analysis of Isaiah 52:13–53:12 in his monograph, *Disability and Isaiah's Suffering Servant* (Schipper 2011). Of course, this passage is one of the most famous in the Hebrew Bible, yet it has infrequently been identified as a poem about a person with a disability. Schipper argues persuasively that the figure in the passage is an individual with a disability (Schipper 2011, 31–59). Schipper describes disability as "the social and political experience of impairment" (Schipper 2011, 31). He explores the specific linguistic terms used to describe the servant in 52:13–53:12. The modern author does not try to diagnose the particular malady that the servant has, but he notes that Isaiah 53 attributes Yhwh as the source of the disability, that is, God is represented as "striking" the servant with a disability (53:4; Schipper 2011, 35). Indeed, in 53:10, God is "pleased" to crush the servant by disease.

The issue of God being pictured as the deliberate cause or source of a disability is problematic when interpreting from a perspective of disability. Some people with disabilities truly struggle with the theological premise that God causes disability. Isaiah 52:13–53:12 also represents the servant as bearing other people's punishment for sin. The servant with a disability bears the sins of the community perhaps most famously in 53:5: "He was wounded for our transgressions, crushed for our iniquities; upon him was the punishment that made us whole, and by his bruises we are healed." This, too, can cause consternation for a person with a disability. The idea that a person might be stricken with a disability in order to atone for other people's sins seems innately unfair.

Isaiah 52:14 states that the people were astonished at the servant because his appearance was marred. It is not evident what feature in his visage was startling but there is a reaction to his appearance by many, according to the verse. People with visible disabilities can in some cases relate to people's startled reaction. Verses 2 and 3 of chapter 53 develop the theme of the servant's appearance, emphasizing the lack of appeal and the rejection by others: "He has no form or comeliness that we should look at him; nothing in his appearance that we should desire him. He was despised and rejected by others, a man of suffering and acquainted with grief; and as one from whom others hide their faces, he was despised and we did not esteem him" (vv. 2a–3).

Isaiah 53:7 raises some issues for a disability reading: "He was oppressed and he was afflicted, but he did not open his mouth; like a lamb that was led to the slaughter; and like a sheep that before its shearers is silent, so he did not open his mouth." Though this passage has had spiritual significance for many religious people, it does raise some concerns for our task here. The servant with disability is portrayed as being oppressed and afflicted, but he is silent in the face of that. It could be read as encouraging people with disabilities to acquiesce to oppression and discrimination, to remain silent. However, disability activists would bristle at this idea, preferring to press on to achieve equality. By and large, it seems that the servant exists for the benefit of others, to bear their iniquity and through his righteousness make many righteous (see v. 11). Verse 5a, of course, indicates that "upon him was the punishment that made us whole, and by his bruises we are healed." As Schipper clarifies, "In Isaiah 53, a pious servant figure with unspecified disabilities or illnesses plays a critical role in the redemption of others with no clear indication that he experiences any healing or normalization (cf. 42.7–17)" (Schipper 2015, 326). While bringing redemption to the community, nevertheless the servant deserved a life that satisfied his own needs and desires, as any person with disability deserves a satisfying life.

Feminine metaphors predominate in chapter 54, portraying the city of Jerusalem as the abandoned wife/mother who will be reconciled to her husband, YHWH. The opening in verse 1 draws on the recurring theme in ancient Israel that female infertility is a disability. Women who were unable to bear children experienced shame in that culture. For example, Rachel utters the words, "God has taken away my reproach," in Genesis 30:22 after she gives birth to Joseph (Melcher 2017, 45). Verse 1 of Isaiah 54 addresses the infertile woman: "Sing, O Barren One, who has not borne; burst into song and shout, you who have not been in labor" (v. 1a). The verse ends by promising that the barren one will eventually bear more children than the married woman. There will be numerous descendants, according to the promise of verse 3. Following this, the shame of youth and the disgrace of widowhood will be reversed (v. 4). Though the outcome is promising, these verses reinscribe the cultural judgment that women who do not give birth are subject to shame and rejection.

The reversal comes about because YHWH will be Israel's husband. All will be well due to God's relationship with Israel as woman. The benefits are spelled out in verse 6: "For like a woman forsaken and grieved in spirit, YHWH has called you, like the wife of a man's youth when she is cast off, says your God." Like the rejected and abandoned woman, God has called Israel. Though God had originally abandoned female Israel and hid God's face from her, "with everlasting love, I will have compassion on you, says YHWH, your redeemer" (v. 8). Today we might challenge the idea that infertility is a disability, but the shame associated with it in ancient Israel is also something to be challenged. Whether a woman bears children or not, she is worthy of complete respect as a person of innate value. Though the metaphor of a barren woman is intended to represent the nation of Israel as beleaguered due to the experience of exile, it is demeaning to women to repeat the idea of cultural shame in the face of infertility.

THIRD ISAIAH: CHAPTERS 56–66

Blenkinsopp argues persuasively that the section Third Isaiah, chapters 56–66, does not come from a single author nor from a single time period (Blenkinsopp 2003, 58). The material that has been compiled and placed in this section is quite diverse and most probably was created over time by numerous contributors. There seems to be some dependence upon the section Isaiah 40–55 (Blenkinsopp 2003, 64). Some of the texts from the previous section have been adapted, revised, or expanded to address the concerns of a later generation of Judahites. Blenkinsopp outlines his position about the relationship of chapters 56–66 to 40–55: "We seem to be able to make out in the texts the faint imprint of prophetic and scribal activity carried on over several generations by a movement or school owing allegiance to the prophetic leader and teacher responsible for the core of 40–55 . . ." (Blenkinsopp 2003, 65). Though some scholars have maintained otherwise, Blenkinsopp argues well that there is no necessary connection between Isaiah 56:1–8 and the separationist measures enacted by Ezra and Nehemiah (Blenkinsopp 2003, 142). Yet, if one reads other postexilic passages as possible background for Isaiah 56–66, one can discern a disagreement of policy between the lines, so to speak. There seems to be more than one point of view about how the identity of Judah should be shaped going forward.

Isaiah 56:1–8 is a very inclusive text, reassuring eunuchs and foreigners that they can become members of the Judean postexilic community. According to verses 2 and 4, if one keeps the sabbath, refrains from doing evil, and maintains the covenant, that is all that is required. Most pertinent to our discussion is the focus on inclusion for the eunuch. In ancient Judah, a man who was unable to reproduce, to father children, was considered to have a disability (Melcher 2011, 120–21).

The passage may reflect a conflict surrounding the identity of the postexilic community of Judah. Chapter 56:1–8 takes the approach that those who adhered to the covenant of YHWH could be admitted to the community and allowed to worship in the rebuilt temple (Paul 2012, 448). Yet, the impression gleaned from other postexilic biblical texts is that another faction wanted to define the community more narrowly, as pure of lineage and devoid of foreign influences (see, e.g., Ezra 9:1–2, 12, and 10:11). Third Isaiah speaks out strongly against this desire for "ethnic purity." Indeed, the less inclusive faction promoted reproduction, but sought to define the next generation as descended from the exiles who have returned to Judah. This faction wanted to control reproduction and eunuchs did not fit into the goal of producing future generations, so they were not welcome according to some. Earlier passages such as Deuteronomy 23:2 and Leviticus 21:21 implies that some defects preclude a person's presence in the temple (in the first instance) or prevents their service at the altar (in the second instance).

This section of Isaiah takes on the deeply embedded cultural imperative to reproduce. Verse 3 exhorts the eunuch to refrain from calling himself "a dry tree," a derogatory expression. God has a generous answer to the eunuch's self-defacement: "For thus says YHWH: 'To the eunuchs who keep my sabbaths, who choose the things that please me and hold fast my covenant, I will give, in my house and in my walls, a monument and a name better than sons and daughters, I will give them an everlasting name that will not be cut off'" (vv. 4–5).

Chapter 59 relies on metaphors of disability to craft a contrast between the very able and righteous YHWH and the sinful nation of Judah. Verse 1 states: "No, YHWH's arm is not too short to save, nor his ear too dull to hear." This clarifies that God has no impairment and could save the people if that were appropriate. According to the prophetic voice, the reason vindication has not come is that the people are on the wrong path, but God is ready to save at the appropriate time. The subsection, Isaiah 59:9–15a, constitutes a confession of wrongdoing by the people of Judah and metaphors of disability are used to illustrate their lost and misguided state: "We grope like the blind along a wall, groping like those who have no eyes. We stumble at noon as in the twilight, we are like dead people among the vigorous" (v. 10). Further physical metaphors make the case that the people have not been faithful: "Transgressing and denying YHWH and turning away from following our God, speaking oppression and revolt, conceiving lying words and uttering them from the heart" (v. 13). Another metaphor of disability occurs in verse 14b, where "truth stumbles in the public square and uprightness cannot enter."

We have seen this use of physical metaphors to describe the sinfulness and wrongdoing of God's people of Judah before. In chapter 59 they are intended to describe the people as headed in the wrong direction, as wandering from the path. The metaphors of blindness are intended to indicate Judah's inability to find their way, or at least their difficulty in doing so. The metaphor of truth stumbling in the square uses physical metaphor to indicate moral laxity. People in Judah cannot seem to live by the covenant requirements to be truthful and live justly. Nevertheless, the use of these metaphor casts people with disabilities in a negative light, as illustrating the lack of a firm sense of faithfulness and an ability to head in a direction devoted to God.

The woman in labor motif occurs again in chapter 66, in a passage that envisions a great transformation. When the exiles are restored to Zion, a woman shall give birth before she experiences labor and deliver a son before she feels pain (v. 7). This time the woman in labor is Zion itself who will deliver her children in a moment (v. 8). Verse 9 depicts God's power over labor and birth: "Shall I open the womb and not deliver, says YHWH? Shall I, the one who delivers, shut the womb? Says YHWH." In this case, the woman has extraordinary powers in the birth process, she who delivers without pain has powers beyond any other woman. This miracle occurs because of the great transformation of Zion.

THEOLOGICAL IMPLICATIONS

Isaiah 1 portrays God as an abusive parent, who has beaten the child Israel for her/his rebellion. Israel has been beaten so badly that there are open sores all over her/his body. The imagery is rather brutal and the land itself is left desolate, "like a shelter in a cucumber field" (v. 8). The reason for the beating is the child's rebellion, but surely the depiction of God as abusive is disturbing from either a feminist perspective or through a disability lens. Perhaps this passage could be contrasted with Hosea 11, where God as parent is presented as being unable to give up God's child. In this chapter of Hosea, God's love holds the divine back from handing Israel over (v. 8). There God recoils from causing harm and is filled with compassion. In the following verse God refrains from coming in wrath (v. 9). This juxtaposition of Hosea 11 with Isaiah 1 presents an unbreakable bond between God and child Israel, which prevails.

Chapter 1 of Isaiah reminds us of the holiness of God, that God is Holy Other. This Holy One of Israel calls for the nation's people to purify themselves by ceasing to do evil, to learn to do good (v. 16). The people were to "seek justice, rescue the oppressed, defend the orphan, plead for the widow" (v. 17). Though verse 17 speaks for justice for the oppressed, the orphan, and the widow, these are representative figures, not elements in an exhaustive list. This exhortation is in keeping with a call to seek justice for people with disabilities, and for people of all genders. The requirement for seeking justice is a very positive aspect of Isaiah 1, as it shows the authors' interest in inculcating a sense of justice in readers of the text.

Ironically, an aspect of holiness that may help to limit the gap between God and people is its base meaning of being "set apart." People can be "set apart" in order to serve God in a particular capacity. In fact, some people can be consecrated ("made holy") to signify their calling to a divinely given task. In the case of Isaiah 1, perhaps the people are cleansed in order to fulfill the divine exhortation to pursue justice.

Chapter 4's reference to women and their menstrual blood as connoting moral impurity is difficult. Ancient Israel saw menstrual blood as generating a form of ritual impurity making it necessary for menstruating women to be absent from the cult. This conferring of ritual impurity on a natural process is troubling enough, but to associate menstruation with a lack of moral fitness is more difficult. While the passage deals with this bodily function in a metaphorical way, the focus on women and their menstruation is troubling and may reflect some cultural stereotypes.

Many passages in Isaiah speak of God's sovereignty. It is important to keep in mind that God is powerful and that power can be restorative and transformative. Yet, though Isaiah presents God as capable of making the ground level, as having limitless transformative power, all of us know that not everyone is physically healed by the power of God. In fact, sometimes our disabilities are an integral part of us, inextricably intertwined with our identity. This point is made effectively in *Theology and Down Syndrome*, where the author retells a story of a woman with Down syndrome who asks if she will be healed of that condition when she gets to heaven. Her parents indicate that she will be healed, but the woman asks, "'But, how will you know me then?'" (Yong 2007, 259; Gaventa and Coulter 2003, 132).

As I noted above, God's holiness and powerful sovereignty can create a distance between God and the people. Yet there are theological concepts that remind us of intimacy and closeness to God. For instance, Isaiah 50:8 declares, "The One who justifies me is near. Who will contend with me? Let us stand together. Who are my adversaries? Let them confront me." Psalm 73:28 states, "But as for me, it is good for me to be near God. I have put my trust in the Lord YHWH that I may declare all your works." Numerous passages speak to the nearness of God and it is good to keep God's nearness in mind when we also consider the sovereignty and holiness of God, for God can also be accessible.

Of course, Isaiah 2 speaks of YHWH's sovereignty as ushering in peace among the nations. This chapter provides a vision of the future where swords were beaten into plowshares and spears into pruning hooks. Indeed, all the nations are depicted as wanting to learn about God. Certainly, this potential for peace is something positive for all people including people with disabilities and people of all genders. The potential for peace is especially notable because disability is often created in war. As the National Park Service has observed, "war inevitably means some soldiers will come home with short-term or long-lasting disabilities" (Meldon n.d.).

Oftentimes in Isaiah moral failure or sinfulness is portrayed in terms of impaired physical mobility. In particular, the portrayal of people stumbling on the path or wandering away from the path is used frequently in Isaiah. Military defeat is often depicted in terms of stumbling and falling. As noted above, the equating of moral failing, sinfulness, unfaithfulness, and military defeat to mobility impairment is difficult for those with physical disabilities. Perhaps these portrayals can be mitigated somewhat with biblical passages such as Isaiah 40:11, "He will feed his flock like a shepherd; he will gather the lambs in his arms, and carry them in his bosom, and gently lead the mother sheep." There are numerous passages in Isaiah and in the other prophets that emphasize God's compassion and the divine impetus to care, the providential aspect of God.

Other chapters use physical metaphors to convey moral failure as well. This type of rhetoric is effective, particularly in ancient times, because they use images with which all can identify. Isaiah 6 is a case in point, because the prophet's lips become the vehicle to describe sinfulness: "Woe is me! I am lost, for I am a man of unclean lips and I live among a people of unclean lips; yet my eyes have seen the King, Yhwh of hosts" (v. 5). Physical impurity and moral failing go hand in hand. This kind of metaphor brings the idea of sinfulness home to the listener because of the immediacy that physical metaphors provide. They are rooted in ancient people's environs and are easily relatable, but they also can denigrate the body part they represent.

The book of Isaiah in several instances uses degrading metaphors of women to illustrate Judah's arrogance or its desperate plight. The passage in Isaiah 3:16–26 would be more acceptable if there were a similar passage that describes the male inhabitants of Judah as haughty and arrogant in an extended way, as occurs here in reference to women. In a patriarchal society, it is more acceptable to use metaphors of marginalized groups to portray the people as arrogant and disrespectful toward God. However, to single out women or people with disabilities to illustrate bad attitudes or wrongful behavior is to reinforce disparaging attitudes toward women and people with disabilities. Chapter 4 portrays women as experiencing shame because they do not have husbands or sons to lend them status. This is deprecating to women. Better to portray women as having their own innate value in society independent from their relationship to a male head of household. Also, Isaiah 4:4 contains an allusion to menstrual blood as a symbol of moral impurity. This is derogatory language about a natural, healthy process.

Isaiah 19:16 implies that women stereotypically are more susceptible to fearfulness than men, as Egyptians are depicted as fearful, like women. A number of passages in Isaiah use the metaphor of a woman in labor to depict abject fear on the part of the people of Judah: Isaiah 13:8a, 21:3, 26:17 (cf. 42:14, 45:10). Although the mortality rate for women in labor was high in ancient Israel and Judah, so that women had reason to be fearful when in labor, these passages use the woman in labor metaphor to characterize people as extremely fearful (Kalmanofsky 2008, 66; Frymer-Kensky 1992, 97). It is a stereotypical metaphor and it is demeaning to women. It would be better if there were passages that counter the stereotypical ones. At any rate, part of a feminist approach is to point out demeaning passages and not allow them to stand unchallenged. This portrayal of childbirth should not be attributed to men's ignorance of the facts of childbirth, since John Makujina argues for their competence in this matter (Makujina 2016).

An interesting idea to consider when analyzing Isaiah's use of metaphors of women and of people with disabilities, is Carole Fontaine's theory that feminine gender was a disability in the ancient world (Fontaine 2007). In these passages of Isaiah, women and people with disabilities share a reduced status in the perspectives of the Isaianic authors. This may reflect a cultural situation in ancient Judah where women were considered second-class citizens, of reduced status according to societal standards.

While the concept of the sovereignty of God in Isaiah embraces the aspect of redemption, restoration, and transformation, there may be some issues even with these positive attributes. Isaiah portrays God as someone who enlists the aid of an Assyrian/Babylonian emperor and his army to punish God's recalcitrant people and the book also depicts God as removing disability. Isaiah's God has the power to restore the exiles to the land and to radically transform their circumstances. Yet, one still has to grapple with the idea that God does not always cure disabilities in modern circumstances. Hans S. Reinders suggests another way in which God's providence might be transformative. "Providence, to cut a long story short, is about how the love that God sends into our lives guides us in discovering a new self, the self that finds itself at the other side of the chasm and, in that sense, is transformed to receive a new future. This is the provision God makes through the presence of the Spirit" (Reinders 2014, 180).

In a few cases in Isaiah, as noted above, Judah's enemies are depicted as having idealized strength and stamina. The enemy from the north is pictured as of such enormous power that it is futile to resist those armies. When juxtaposed with metaphors of weakness or disability, that puts the enemy at an impossible advantage. While it is true that Assyria's or Babylon's resources were far greater than

Judah's, since they were massive empires, depictions of them as super powerful makes the contrast with women and the disabled that much more significant.

Chapter 5 is one of the passages in which someone is depicted with extraordinary power, beyond human capacity. It is one thing to portray YHWH possessing astonishing power; it is another to portray other humans in that fashion. In this case, the Assyrian military is portrayed as having greater than expected human strength. They do not tire, and they move swiftly from Assyria to Judah. The poem represents Judah's enemies like fierce lions who roar over their prey and then carry them off, a fitting representation for military forces from Assyria who threaten the kingdoms of Israel and Judah. Yet, the poem instills a deep fear. The enemies are strong, not subject to fatigue, their footwear does not wear out, and their ferociousness knows no bounds. These are unrealistic portrayals, but they make the point that the enemy is powerful and headed toward Judah. This is very effective rhetoric to warn the people of an impending attack by the Assyrians. The book of Isaiah is known for using rhetoric that would impact the ancient hearers.

Isaiah does work on providing a new vision of the future, a vision of a restored Judah. The book attempts to shape a transformation of thinking on the part of the reader, seeing God as a redeemer who will enable the exiles to return. Following Reinders's lead, perhaps the reader can accept a vision of the future that is restorative, changing a firmly held attitude. In addition, some visions of restoration envision pregnant women, women in labor, and people with disabilities at the head of the procession of returnees. While this repeats the pattern of making people with disabilities objects to illustrate God's power, it also portrays them as leaders of the restoration.

2

"Their Ears Are Closed"

The Book of Jeremiah

In the previous chapter, the discussion focused on the sovereignty/providence of God related to metaphors about disability. This chapter on Jeremiah will explore these same relationships, exploring the sovereignty or providence of God in relationship to disability metaphors.

Following up on Carole Fontaine's suggestion that feminine gender was a disability in ancient Israel, this chapter will include some exploration of the use of images in Jeremiah about women (Fontaine 2007). This chapter will also explore some similarities between the treatment of the women and people with disabilities in the text of Jeremiah.

Like Isaiah, Jeremiah probably was written, compiled, and edited in stages. The ancient versions of Jeremiah reflect much variety among them. In particular, there is a significant difference in length between the traditional Hebrew text (the Masoretic Text) and the ancient Greek version (the Septuagint). The Septuagint version of Jeremiah is one-eighth shorter than the Masoretic Text and the second half of the book is arranged differently between the two versions (Coogan 2014, 366).

The first section, chapters 1–25, consists primarily of poetic oracles confronting Judah, Jerusalem, the people, and their rulers, though there is also some prose narrative. Some scholars regard this section as the first scroll that Jeremiah dictated to Baruch (Coogan

2014, 367). Chapters 26–29 contain narratives telling of Jeremiah's conflicts with other prophets and members of the establishment. Often called "the book of consolation," chapters 30–33 share affinities with Second Isaiah with frequent comforting oracles. The next section, chapters 34–45, are prose narratives dating primarily to the reign of Zedekiah and the time after the fall of Jerusalem in 586 BCE. Chapters 46–51 contain oracles against the nations, similarly to oracles against the nations in Amos, Isaiah, and Ezekiel. Jeremiah 52 narrates the fall of Jerusalem and the catastrophic events that followed.

Most scholars discern a Deuteronomic editorial hand in the book. A few chapters in Jeremiah duplicate chapters found in the Deuteronomistic History: Jeremiah 52 duplicates 2 Kings 25 and 2 Kings 18–20 is reproduced in Jeremiah 36–39. Jeremiah's prophetic career likely spanned 627 BCE (King Josiah's thirteenth year) up to several years after the fall of Jerusalem (586 BCE). Of course, events in Josiah's reign inspired growth in the Deuteronomic school, so it is no surprise to discern that influence in the book of Jeremiah. However, William L. Holladay argues that Jeremiah was born in 627 BCE and that he did not begin his prophetic work at that time. Holladay suggests that this explains why there is no clear argument against or in favor of Josiah's reform (Holladay 1986, 1). Most scholars, however, see the date of 627 BCE as the beginning of Jeremiah's work.

CHAPTERS 1–25

In Jeremiah, chapter 1, Yhwh declares through the prophet: "Before I formed you in the womb, I knew you, and before you were born, I consecrated you; I appointed you a prophet to the nations" (v. 5). This verse establishes Jeremiah's status as a prophet (Carroll 2004, 78). Yhwh shapes the prophet and his vocation from the beginning, using metaphorical language that may remind the listener of the work of a potter (cf. Genesis 2:7). This is a very physical representation of how Yhwh set Jeremiah apart to do prophecy on behalf of Yhwh. In verse 6 Jeremiah resists the call from Yhwh, complaining that he did not know how to speak. The following verse makes it clear that Yhwh controls where Jeremiah will go and what he will speak: "Do not say 'I am only a boy'; for you shall go to all to whom I send you, and you shall speak whatever I command you" (v. 7).

Verse 9 illustrates Yʜwʜ's "hands on" approach: "The Yʜwʜ put out his hand and touched my mouth; and Yʜwʜ said to me, 'Now I have put my words in your mouth'" (v. 9). According to Jeremiah 1, the divine put words into Jeremiah's mouth, physically determining what Jeremiah shall say. Later in the chapter, Yʜwʜ promises to be with Jeremiah, protecting him from the people, making Jeremiah a fortified city, an iron pillar, and a bronze wall. Jeremiah is made strong through Yʜwʜ's presence (O'Connor 2011, 72). The passage impresses the listener with the idea that God has power over speech and can lend the prophet intestinal fortitude in the face of resistance.

Jeremiah chapter 3 certainly employs metaphors about women to call Judah back to fidelity with God. Verse 1 draws from Deuteronomy 24:1–4 and possibly Hosea 2 to describe the situation in which a man divorces a woman, then she becomes the wife of another man (Holladay 1986, 112). If the second man dies or divorces her, may the first man make her his wife again? God is portrayed as asking this same question about Israel, saying, "'You have whored with many lovers: can you return to me?' says Yʜwʜ" (v. 1b). Verse 2 illustrates Israel's behavior in very demeaning terms, picturing her as waiting by the roadside for men with whom she could copulate, that is, "like a bandit." The land was defiled by Israel's behavior and "she had the forehead of a harlot," indicating her stubbornness (v. 3). Turning to prose narrative in verse 6, the passage uses the familiar phrase, "On every high hill and under every green tree, she has acted the whore there" (cf. Deut 12:2; 1 Kgs 14:23; 2 Kgs 16:4, 17:10; Jer 2:20; Ezek 6:13). God thought that Israel would return to God, but instead "her sister Judah" engaged in the same behavior. Judah engaged in faithless behavior and only pretended to return to God. C. L. Crouch argues persuasively that "rebellious Israel is meant to signify the community exiled to Babylonia, while Traitorous Judah represents those left behind in the land" (Crouch 2020, 603). This solves some of the interpretive problems that have plagued scholars analyzing this passage.

In spite of Israel's unfaithfulness, Yʜwʜ indicates that divine mercy is available to her. God will not be angry forever (v. 12). However, God requires that she confess her wrongdoing and repent (v. 13). Then, the passage incorporates the parental metaphors for the relationship between God and the people. The people then become faithless children, but spousal metaphors remain: "'Return, rebellious children,' says Yнwн, 'for I am married to you; I will take you, one from a city and two from a family, and I will bring you to Zion'" (v. 14). Through this mixed use of metaphors, the passage expresses the unbreakable bond between children and parent or between husband and wife. Those who have been estranged will be reunited in Zion. Yet, while expressing an unbreakable bond, it implies that the stronger party will impose the divine will upon the spouse and child. The implication is that the people of Israel may be reunited with God against their will. These sisters, Israel and Judah, raise anxieties in the reader because of their promiscuity and unfaithfulness to God and also because of their sisterly bond (Kalmanofsky 2011). These anxieties may be intended to incite horror for the audience so that they will reform (Kalmanofsky 2011, 304–5).

Verses 15–18 of Jeremiah 3 envision a restoration of Zion in which God provides good leaders for the people, who follow God's heart. The people will increase in the land and all the nations will be gathered to God in Jerusalem. The passage imagines a time when Israel and Judah have returned from the north and are reunited in the land. While this is a vision for a promising future, there is also the allusion to the people's obedience to the divine will (v. 17).

However, verses 19 and 20 return to a mixture of parental and spousal metaphors to upbraid the people of Judah for their unfaithfulness. Once again, the people of Judah are portrayed as rebellious children and an unfaithful wife. Verses 21 and 22 return to the rebellious children metaphors portraying children who refuse to return to God the father. The end of the chapter, verses 22–25, pictures the children acknowledging their recalcitrance and confessing their transgressions against God, yet also returning fully to the fold. They cry out in shame, admitting their disobedience.

The metaphors of Jeremiah 3 leave the reader with the sense of a God who insists on obedience from God's people and who exerts pressure to encourage the people to return and adhere to the divine will. This reader feels somewhat ill at ease with God's metaphorical anger and angst with children and spouse. Reflected in this passage is the hierarchy extant in the culture, where males are very powerful, but children and women are disobedient and immoral, and God is the most powerful of all. This is a deity who holds the people accountable for deviating from the divine will.

Though chapter 4 of Jeremiah does not have an abundance of disability metaphors in it, the end of the chapter has a striking metaphor of Zion as a woman in childbirth. Verses 30–31 employ feminine imagery of Judah as she awaits her punishment through the enemies from the north: "O you who are plundered, what do you accomplish by wearing crimson, that you deck yourself with gold ornaments, that you enlarge your eyes with paint? In vain you beautify yourself; your lovers despise you, they seek your life. For I have heard a voice like a woman in labor, anguish like one bringing forth her first child, the cry of daughter Zion gasping for breath, stretching out her hands, 'Alas for me, I faint before killers'" (vv. 30–31). This passage again uses feminine metaphors to paint a negative picture of Judah under siege. The writer denigrates women who dress in crimson and who wear eye makeup because there are "lovers" entering the land to plunder the people. The metaphor of a woman in labor is used to indicate that Judah is vulnerable to attack. The writers have used feminine metaphors to express negative aspects of the populace, implying their unfaithfulness, vanity, and immorality. This denigrates an oppressed group in order to symbolize the culpability of the entire nation.

Chapter 5, verse 7 expresses Judah's unfaithfulness using metaphors about children. The verse also describes Judah's unfaithfulness in terms of an unfaithful spouse: "How can I pardon you? Your children have forsaken me, and have sworn by those who are not gods. When I had fed them to the full, they committed adultery, and they trooped to the houses of prostitutes" (v. 7). Though children are depicted as unfaithful, the imagery now depicts men as unfaithful with prostitutes. God is compelled to punish because of their behavior (v. 9).

In a declaration in 5:20–22, the passage addresses both Israel and Judah and calls them foolish and senseless people, "who have eyes but do not see; ears but do not hear" (v. 21). These disability metaphors, which connote non-functioning eyes and ears, describe people who have turned away from God and who do not return. Verse 23 uses another physical metaphor to convey the same idea: "This people have a stubborn and rebellious heart; they have turned aside and gone away." These physical metaphors compare alienation from God and deliberate distance from God in terms of a disability. The moral failure is located in the eyes, ears, and heart.

Jeremiah 6:10 uses sensory disability metaphors to indicate Judah's obstinance and refusal to follow God's instructions: "To whom shall I speak and give warning, that they may hear? See, their ears are closed, they cannot listen, the word of YHWH is a reproach to them, they take no delight in it." The Hebrew term translated as "closed" here may be more accurately rendered as "uncircumcised," which would constitute a disability among a people for whom circumcision is a requirement (Couey 2017, 243). Yet, the overwhelming sense of this verse is that an inability to hear is equated with recalcitrance, a refusal to listen to and then follow God. A similar motif appears in verse 19: "Hear, O Earth! I am going to bring disaster upon this people, the fruit of their own schemes, because they have not given heed to my words; they rejected my instruction." God calls earth as witness to hear the prediction of disaster for the people, because they have not heeded God's words by obeying God's teaching. Thus, the metaphor of hearing connotes obedience to God, while being unable or unwilling to hear implies noncompliance with God's teaching.

Another familiar motif recurs in chapter 6, when verse 23 refers to daughter Zion and the following verse describes the people's anguish and pain, likening their experience to that of a woman in labor. Verse 24 also refers to hands that fall helpless in the fear of the warriors from the north. Again, feminine metaphors are used to convey the negative feelings of those facing imminent destruction.

Of course, the idols of the nations are denigrated for their lack of ability or effectiveness. Chapter 10, verse 5 is a case in point: "They are like a scarecrow in a cucumber field, they cannot speak. They have to be carried, because they cannot walk. Be not afraid of them, for they can do no harm. Nor is it in them to do any good." Verses 6 and 7 emphasize that God is incomparable and that the gods of the nations do not even come close. The following verses 10–17 make the same kind of comparisons between God and the idols. God's power in creating the earth is contrasted with the inabilities of the idols and their unreality as gods.

In an unusual reference, Jeremiah 12:4 implies that God cannot or does not see, but this refers to the wicked who persist in their sinfulness because they say to themselves that God does not see them. The passage intends to refute that notion, arguing that God will see to their punishment. Listing in detail the terrible things that will happen to the evildoers, the passage clarifies that God has control over the present and the future, with the future looking especially grim.

Chapter 13, verse 16 uses the motif of stumbling in the dark to illustrate what God will do to the unrepentant: "Give glory to YHWH your God before he brings darkness, before your feet stumble on the mountains at twilight; while you hope for light, he turns it into gloom, and he makes it deep darkness." Once the stumbling in the dark takes place, the people will be taken into captivity, according to verse 17. Verses 21 and 22 use feminine imagery to illustrate just how bad this payback will be. Judah will be like a woman in labor because of the pain the people will experience when enemies overrun their land. Because of Judah's iniquity, "your skirts will be lifted up and you are violated" (v. 22b). Metaphors of violent rape are used to indicate how terrible Judah's punishment will be for their transgressions. This is a very difficult metaphor for anyone who has experienced sexual violation or harassment. Lest the people of Judah blame the Babylonians for their violation, YHWH makes it clear who will be responsible for this act in verse 26: "I myself will lift your skirt over your face and your shame will be seen." The metaphor of God preparing a woman for rape is disturbing, though it is intended to indicate how severe Judah's punishments will be for her recalcitrance and unfaithfulness.

Jeremiah 14:9 is initially accusative of God: "Why should you be like someone confused, like a mighty warrior who is unable to save. Yet, you, YHWH, are in the midst of us; we are called by your name. Do not forsake us!" In Hebrew laments, sometimes God is accused of hiding the divine face or of abandoning the people. Here, God is accused of acting like God is mentally confused and unable to save the people. Usually, this kind of accusation is followed by an assurance that God is faithful, and that is the case in verse 9, when God's presence among the people is acknowledged.

As we saw in this book's chapter 1 concerning Isaiah, Jeremiah uses metaphors of straying from a path as indicative of Judah's unfaithfulness. For example, in Jeremiah 14:10: "Thus says YHWH concerning this people; 'Truly they have loved to wander, they have not restrained their feet; therefore, YHWH does not accept them, now he will remember their iniquity and punish their sins." Chapter 14 concludes with the people of Judah pleading with God, confessing their transgressions, exhorting God to care about the divine reputation, and expressing confidence that God will ultimately save them (see vv. 19–22).

Once again, in chapter 15, metaphors of women are employed to describe convincingly Judah's impending fate. The relevant verses are part of a lament in 15:5–9 and suggests a situation where God is "both slayer of the community and its chief mourner" (Carroll 2004, 45). In verse 8, widows become as numerous as the sand of the sea and mothers of youths face a destroyer. Verse 9 continues the use of feminine metaphors to portray the utter violent defeat of Judah. The mother of seven faints, the sun goes down on her, then she is shamed and disgraced. In the following verse 10, the prophet cries out with, "Woe to me, my mother, that you have borne me a man of strife and a man of contention to all the land. I have not lent, nor have I borrowed, yet all of them curse me" (v. 10).

In Jeremiah 20:7–13, the prophet launches into his most scathing accusations about God's conduct toward him. According to Jeremiah, Yhwh has seduced him into his prophetic vocation, raped him, and prevailed against him (v. 7; O'Connor 2011, 87). During this last of Jeremiah's laments, the motif of stumbling reappears in chapter 20, verses 10 and 11. In the midst of a section that gives "a glimmer of faith's resurgence (20:7–13)," Jeremiah uses this familiar motif (O'Connor 2011, 84). The prophet states in verse 10 a response to overheard whispers: "All my close friends are watching for me to stumble . . . ." Jeremiah imagines that when these so-called friends witness his stumbling, they will begin to plot against him. Moving into the hymn of confidence (vv. 11–13), as Jeremiah continues to visualize, verse 11 reverses the situation, so that the prophet's persecutors would be the ones to stumble (Carroll 2004, 46). Nevertheless, Jeremiah reaffirms his faith that God will be present with him throughout his struggles. However, in both instances (vv. 10 and 11), a physical weakness is used to indicate a moral lapse. A stumble in this context may imply initially that Jeremiah has let his guard down and has not proved to be a true prophet. Yet, his persecutors turn out to be the those who have stumbled and plotted against Yhwh's prophet.

While one of the intents of chapter 22 may be to give the reader a glimpse of a useless king, it is distinguished by its presentation of justice concerns (Kidner 2014, 84). The first nine verses appear to be addressed to King Jehoiakim, a son of Josiah (Kidner 2014, 86). As

Robert P. Carroll points out, "a very general deuteronomistic piece in 22.1–5 ties the security of the city/palace/temple . . . into the ethical behavior of the royal house (cf. the temple sermon in 7.5–7)" (Carroll 2004, 49). Verse 3 looks like a précis of what constitutes covenant adherence: "Thus says YHWH, 'Act with justice and righteousness, and deliver from the hand of the oppressor anyone who has been robbed. And do no wrong or violence to the alien, the orphan, and the widow, or shed innocent blood in this place.'" If the king does follow these standards, then kings will continue to sit on the throne of David. If not, then the kingdom of Judah will be destroyed (vv. 6–9). The failure to live up to the covenant is cited in verse 9 as a reason for the destruction.

Later in chapter 22, verses 13–19, King Jehoiakim is taken to task for his failure to pursue justice and he is compared unfavorably in that regard to his father Josiah. Verses 20–23 appear to address a feminine figure, probably Jerusalem, and she is told that her lovers will go into captivity. She will suffer when the Babylonians raze the city, and she will groan when the pain of childbirth comes upon her (v. 23). It is significant that this feminine metaphor of pain in childbirth shows up so frequently to depict the degradation of the city and its suffering.

Chapter 23 of Jeremiah takes issue at some length with the leaders of ancient Judah, with the "shepherd," kings, and prophets. As Jeremiah confronts the other prophets, he uses physical metaphors to convey his anguish at their behavior: "Concerning the prophets: my heart is crushed within me, all my bones are shaking, I have become like a drunkard, like one overcome by wine, because of YHWH, and because of his holy words" (v. 9). This physical description is compelling and illustrates the depth of Jeremiah's agony over the behavior of the false prophets. Yet the association of physical instability with drunkenness is disturbing when looking at the passage through a disability lens. Jeremiah 23 brings up again the theme of wrong or difficult paths where a person's footing is unsure. Later in verse 11, Jeremiah continues listing his displeasure with the prophets, stating that "their way of running is evil" (Baumgartner and Koehler 2001, 634). Verse 12 deals with the failure of the prophets to provide faithful leadership to the people of Judah: "'Therefore their way shall be to them like slippery paths in the darkness, into which they shall be driven and fall; for I will bring disaster upon them in the year of their punishment,' says

Yʜwʜ." The theme of how people move about and the theme of straying from the good path arises several times throughout Jeremiah. To Jeremiah and Isaiah, there is one good path that people should follow, the path that leads to God. Straying from the path or finding the path difficult to traverse is symbolic of failure to keep to God's covenant, God's way of life. That is a problematic way to express a lack of faithfulness for those whose disability impacts their mobility.

Jeremiah 25 presents strongly a theme of God's sovereignty. The chapter focuses primarily on God's power to punish all the nations, including Judah. The metaphor of the wine of wrath illustrates God's sovereignty to punish very well. Verses 15–16 reads, "For thus Yʜwʜ, God of Israel, said to me: 'Take from my hand this cup of the wine of wrath, and make all the nations to whom I send you drink it. They shall drink and stagger and go out of their minds because of the sword that I am sending among them.'" The phrase "go out of their minds" could alternatively be rendered as "act madly" (Olyan 2008, 69). Jeremiah took the cup from God and made the nations drink it. The remainder of the chapter portrays the destruction that ensues, brought through divine will. For every nation and its leaders, God shall be "like a lion he has left his culvert; for their land has become a waste because of the cruel sword, and because of his fierce anger" (v. 38). Included among the nations who will be punished is Babylon, for God is sovereign over them as well (O'Connor 2011, 117).

CHAPTERS 26–29

Jeremiah 27 establishes the sovereignty of God very clearly, especially in verse 5, in which God's message to the nations' envoys is given: "It is I who made the earth and the people and animals who are on the earth, by my great might and my outstretched arm, and I give it to whomever I deem proper." God indicates in the following verse that King Nebuchadnezzar of Babylon, servant of Yʜwʜ, will be the recipient and that even the animals will serve him. Those nations who will not serve Nebuchadnezzar will be under siege by Yʜwʜ's hand (v. 8). However, any nation that submits to Babylon will be left on its own soil. The rest of the chapter makes clear that there will be disastrous consequences if Judah resists Babylonian hegemony.

CHAPTERS 30–33

Of course, God's sovereignty or providence means that God can restore Judah and bring the exiles back to the land, as is recorded in chapter 30. In verse 3, the process of restoration is described: "For days are coming, declares Yʜwʜ, when I will restore the fortunes of my people, Israel and Judah, declares Yʜwʜ, and I will bring them back to the land that I gave to their ancestors, and they shall possess it." Without hesitation, God indicates that God possesses the power to bring people out of captivity in Babylon and to restore them to their land.

Yet, to indicate the terror of siege and captivity, the writer uses the metaphor of a woman in labor, but with a new twist: "Ask now and see, can a man bear a child? Why then do I see every man with his hands on his loins like a woman in labor? Why has every face turned pale?" (v. 6). The metaphor of a woman in labor once again serves to communicate the fearfulness of a people awaiting desolation by the Babylonian warriors. As L. Juliana Claassens puts it, "by applying this metaphor to the strong men of the community, this text vividly captures the utter panic and desperation experienced by the people" (Claassens 2014, 68). God describes the day when that happens as distressing, yet Jacob will be rescued by God (v. 7). Though restoration is promised and God will deliver, Judah will not go unpunished (v. 11).

In order to drive home Judah's predicament, the writer uses metaphors of physical injury in verses 12 and 13: "Thus says Yʜwʜ, 'Your affliction is incurable, your wound severe. There is no one to plead your cause, no medicine for your wound, no healing for you.'" Metaphors of physical injury are invoked to convey the hopelessness of Judah's situation. Punishment is inevitable, because of Judah's sickness and guilt. For those who have incurable wounds, the picture of God as an unrelenting foe is difficult to swallow (v. 14). Judah will experience pain in all this, pain that does not dissipate (v. 15). Eventually, however, God will heal the wounds and restore Judah's health (v. 17). God's sovereignty/providence is so great that Judah's kingly succession will be reestablished (v. 21) and the very basis of the covenant will be maintained: "And you will be my people, and I will be your God" (v. 22).

Jeremiah 31 promises that the exiles will return to Judah, but it does not promise healing for those who are disabled (Schipper 2015,

321–22; Couey 2017, 245). Verse 8 describes the people who will be coming back to the land: "See I am going to bring them from the land of the north, and gather them from the farthest parts of the earth, among them the blind and the lame, those with child, and those in labor, together; a great company, they shall return here." Holladay argues that the groups named here "are handicapped, who hinder the easy migration of people" (Holladay 1989, 184). Claassens posits a more felicitous interpretation, that the use of metaphors of the pregnant women and the women in labor evoke the idea of birth or rebirth of the people who return to the land (Claassens 2014, 72). In other words, God will create something new in the restoration. This society reborn will be led by the vulnerable, the blind and the lame, to create something new in the land. Though this is an evocative image, in some ways, it does emphasize the power of God in contrast to the so-called weakness of the blind, the lame, the pregnant, and the woman in labor. Claassens suggests that the fact that these metaphors are used in the middle of the book suggests how tentative the process of recovery could be for those returning from exile (Claassens 2014, 73). Rebecca Raphael notes that the blind and the lame are grammatically male here (Raphael 2011, 113). It is clear that both genders are included in the restored community. Raphael also makes it clear that the changes are to the environment, not to the disabled bodies (Raphael 2011, 114).

The restored Judah will be fertile, as the returnees gather on Mt. Zion, enjoying the bounty of the land, the grain, the wine, the oil, and the meat from flocks and herds (v. 12). As the end of verse 12 puts it, "Their life shall become like a watered garden, and they shall never languish again." There will be much joy and rejoicing among the people (v. 13). Yet, throughout chapter 31, there are alternating swings between restoration and destruction/exile. Again, in verse 15, there is a female metaphor of grief, "A voice is heard in Ramah, lamentation and bitter weeping. Rachel is weeping for her children; she refuses to be comforted for her children, because they are no more." A feminine metaphor of a mother who has lost her children conveys the depth of anguish on the part of the people, as a result of the experience of war, exile, and captivity.

CHAPTERS 34–45

Of interest to this study is the dispute between Jeremiah and the worshipers of the Sovereign of Heaven in Jeremiah 44. In rendering the title of the accused group in this way, I am following the suggestion by Teresa Ann Ellis that the word מלכת may be translated as "sovereign" especially from the perspective of the accused group (Ellis 2009, 467). From Jeremiah's perspective, Ellis suggests translating the phrase as "Queen of Heaven" (Ellis 2009, 467). A change in vowel pointing of this feminine form מלכת means that each of the protagonists can address the issue of the female deity using slightly different terminology.

From verse 9 on in chapter 44 there are gendered arguments about the transgressions of the refugees in Egypt: "Have you forgotten the evil deeds of your ancestors, the crimes of the kings of Judah and their wives, your own misdeeds and those of your wives, which they committed in the land of Judah and in the streets of Jerusalem?" The accusation emphasizes the misdeeds of the wives as well as the husbands in the community. The focus includes both men and women in the community of exile in Egypt. As James E. Harding points out, the dispute on one level is about discernment, about which of the two groups is speaking the truth (Harding 2015, 209). Yet, starting with verse 9, the arguments presented are gendered by listing the wives of the kings and the wives of the men of the land, as Harding stipulates, "The sins that have cried out to heaven for vengeance are thus explicitly gendered, and the focus drawn to the relationship between men and women in provoking YHWH to anger" (Harding 2015, 217). The following verse (v. 10) notes that the people have not been contrite nor have they shown proper reverence. Indeed, they have not followed the teachings and the law that God set before their ancestors.

Verses 11–14 make the case that the exiles in Egypt will suffer the same kind of punishment that has occurred in Judah, ostensibly because of their misdeeds, which were enumerated in previous verses. Following the punishment section of 11–14, verses 15–19 relate the response of the worshipers of the Sovereign of Heaven. All the people of the land, including all the women in the gathering, answer Jeremiah, indicating that they intend to continue making grain offerings to the Sovereign of Heaven. The passage is explicit in its indication that women were present. The people who are gathered accuse Jeremiah of not speaking in Yнwн's name. They argue that when they made the offerings, they had plenty to eat and they prospered without misfortune. When they have failed to make these offerings, they did not have anything to eat and they perished by the sword and by famine. The women also made it clear that their husbands knew that they practiced this form of worship.

Both Ellis and Harding suggest that the worshipers of the Sovereign of Heaven may be arguing that the kind of worship practices in which they have been engaging are legitimate, while Jeremiah, of course, is arguing that they are not legitimate (Ellis 2009, 487; Harding 2015, 218). On the question of punishment, interestingly enough, there is no historical evidence that Nebuchadnezzar causes the wholesale destruction of Pathros in Egypt, though Jeremiah states in verse 28 that if his words stand, that will be proof of him being a true prophet.

The two factions that face off in Jeremiah 44 are gendered as a male prophet representing a male God (Jeremiah/Yнwн) versus a community in which women figure prominently representing a female deity. In point of fact, the issue is not satisfactorily resolved. In some ways, the Jeremiah/Yнwн faction has undercut its own presentation, by making the utter destruction of Pathros and the defeat of Pharaoh Hophra at the hands of Nebuchadnezzar the proof of veracity. The Bible does not report this event nor is there an indication of this coming to pass in other historical sources.

While the male prophet does seek to establish his authority over the men and women worshipers of the Sovereign of Heaven, the women do not fare badly here since Jeremiah fails to make his case against their practices. Yet, there is a gendered conflict embedded within the passage.

CHAPTERS 46–51

In chapter 46, verse 6, we encounter a motif that we have seen several times before; the motif of stumbling and falling. In this case, the passage speaks of a battle between Egypt and Babylon (led by Nebuchadrezzar) at Carchemish. The motif of stumbling and falling expresses the defeat of the Egyptians in battle at the hands of Babylon: "The swift cannot flee away, nor can the warrior escape; in the north by the Euphrates River they have stumbled and fallen" (v. 6).

Defeat in war is symbolized in physical terms, as an inability to walk successfully and falling to the ground. This draws an association of physical disability with defeat, a problematic conceptualization.

This physical stumbling and falling is further characterized in verse 10 as retribution and vindication on the day of YHWH. The verse indicates that God has offered a sacrifice in the land of the north by the River Euphrates. The physical disabling of the Egyptian army is depicted as the direct action of YHWH, God of hosts. Verse 12 repeats the stumbling motif by picturing warrior stumbling against warrior and associates this stumbling with Egypt's shame and crying out. Verse 16 reprises the motif of stumbling in which many people stumble and fall. The association of stumbling with shame is clearly problematic in a disability reading.

In the oracles against Moab in chapter 48, the motif of the woman in labor is used to convey the fear of Moab's warriors: "The towns shall be taken, and the strongholds seized. The hearts of the warriors of Moab, on that day, shall be like the heart of a woman in labor" (v. 41). Presumably the passage compares warriors' fearful hearts to the heart of a woman in labor because she is fearful during the painful birth of her child. It is well worth noting that many women died in childbirth in that historical era. Yet, the passage intends to shame the warrior's fearfulness by comparing this to what a woman feels during childbirth. Nevertheless, the upshot of this is that women are denigrated through the simile. This motif recurs in 49:24, where the anguish and sorrows of Damascus are compared to what a woman in labor goes through.

CHAPTER 52

In examining Jeremiah 52, there is acknowledgement of the direction of borrowing from 2 Kings to the present chapter (Holladay 1989, 439). It seems more likely, as William L. Holladay notes, that the book of Jeremiah added material in verses 10–11 than that 2 Kings abbreviated material from Jeremiah (Holladay 1989, 439). Of course, significantly, the King of Babylon at Riblah slaughtered the sons of Zedekiah "before his eyes," massacred all the officials of Judah, then blinded Zedekiah. Presumably, the greatest set of punishments for the King of Judah was to lose all his sons (thereby destroying the succession to the throne as well as his loved ones) and having that be the last sight Zedekiah sees before being permanently blinded. Zedekiah is then taken in shackles to Babylon where he is kept captive until his death. The phrase, "Put him in the house of milling," found in verse 11, suggests that he was put to work grinding grain, in spite of his blindness (Holladay 1989, 441). Thus, the King of Babylon disables Zedekiah and takes away his freedom. This is in notable contrast to what happens to King Jehoiachin, who, though he is taken hostage to Babylon, is not physically harmed, and in the thirty-seventh year of his exile, is released from prison, receives a stipend, and eats at the table of King Evil-Merodach regularly for the rest of his days (Jeremiah 52:31–34).

In closing this survey section on disability in the prophetic book of Jeremiah, it is useful to look at the closing chapter more closely. In doing so, I draw from the analysis of Adam K. Harger (Harger 2019). In his recent article, he argues that Jeremiah 52 provides the "rhetorical function which validates the experience of the exiles in Babylon" (Harger 2019, 521). Jeremiah urged the Judeans to accept the fact that the Babylonians would soon put them under siege, and to surrender and submit to their oppressors. The Judean kings Jehoiachin and Zedekiah represent someone who surrenders and submits in the first case, then someone who resists in the second case. Jehoiachin lives a long life—treated respectfully by the Babylonian King—then dies in exile in Babylon. However, the King of Babylon has Zedekiah's sons killed before his eyes, then Zedekiah's eyes are put out before he is taken into exile. According to Harger, the chapter is attempting to encourage readers or listeners to surrender and submit to the Babylonians, then they can hope for a similar outcome to Jehoiachin's (Harger 2019, 521–22). A few scholars have pointed to the parallels of going into exile in Babylon to Joseph entering Egypt (Lundbom 2004, 535–37; Harger 2019, 520–22). Another motif that is widely accepted among scholars is the emphasis on the exodus, with the return of the exiles from Babylon as a "new exodus" exceeding the glory of the first. Jeremiah then becomes the new Moses or the (anti-)Moses figure, leading the Judeans out of the Promised Land and into their exilic location in Babylon (Harger 2019, 521). This is very notable for this study because Moses was a prophet with a clear disability.

THEOLOGICAL IMPLICATIONS

Something to keep in mind at the forefront of theological reflection on the treatment of disability in this biblical book is that the writers/compilers of Jeremiah were trying to make sense of a traumatic event in the history of ancient Judah. It would be difficult to exaggerate how deeply distressing the siege and exile by the Babylonians was for the Judeans. As they wrestled with the theological implications, they struggled with understanding God's role in these very difficult circumstances. These authors and editors wanted to value God's providence and sovereignty, so it was more prudent to portray the citizenry as deserving of punishment. Because they wished to preserve God's sovereignty and providential care, the determining factor became whether the people were behaving in a way that conformed to God's will. If the people were disobedient, then punishment (like the siege and exile) would be God's way of calling the people back to the covenant.

However, with the contrast between God the creator and fragile humanity comes a tendency to form a hierarchy or ranking with God at the top, male royalty and priesthood near the top, then males of Judah, women, and people with disabilities. When trying to convey the pain of war and siege, the writer/compilers of the book of Jeremiah often used metaphors of women and of people with disabilities. This would seem to be a relatively safe and effective way to convey Judah's fearfulness and vulnerability, as well as a feeling of powerlessness with a mighty, destructive army threatening at the gates. The goal of conveying Judah's predicament is understandable, but the results of the rhetorical approach are sometimes disparaging to the most marginalized people of ancient Judah's community.

Isaiah 1 and other passages illustrate God's power over the senses and people's bodies. God can put words in people's mouths and cause them to travel to locations of God's choosing. Of course, if God can exercise these powers over people in a way like the depictions in biblical passages, why are some people left without the power of speech? Why do some in Scripture merit God's healing when so many in our current environment are left without that healing? This is a problem with the depiction in Scripture suggesting that God can enhance people's abilities or heal chronic conditions. Not everyone benefits from God's healing power.

Of course, Jeremiah includes hopeful prophecies of how the exiles will be restored to the land and passages that convey God's love for the people of Judah. However, even those passages may use metaphors of pregnant women, women in labor, and people with disabilities to illustrate God's power to redeem people. Unfortunately, this motif reinscribes the hierarchy wherein women and people with disabilities occupy the lower rungs of the ladder. The passages leave the reader with the impression that women and people with disabilities are most in need of God's help to restore Judah to its former glory. The people used in the metaphors are objectified for the sake of proving God's sovereignty and providence over historical events. God has the power to restore all the people and to redeem them from captivity to a foreign power, without exception.

In some ways, it is hard to argue with these redemptive passages. While women and people with disabilities are objectified in order to reveal God's power, these passages also indicate women and people with disabilities will experience full inclusion in the restored community. Perhaps God's special attention to these marginalized people can serve as a rhetorical example that urges the reader to be more inclusive.

The ancient writers/compilers of Jeremiah were attempting to use metaphors that would get the attention of their listeners and readers. That they were successful to a degree is evident in the preservation and dissemination of these ancient texts even today. I do not wish to dismiss the discrimination or objectification of people depicted in these texts, but the writers/compilers were shaped by their social and cultural contexts, and in some ways they were limited by those contexts in the language and rhetorical arguments that they used. Certainly, we still use some of these metaphors in our contemporary context. We, like these ancient authors, are shaped and constrained by our contexts in what we can imagine and express.

A seminal book in the scholarly discourse about disability and theology is Deborah Beth Creamer's work, *Disability and Christian Theology: Embodied Limits and Constructive Possibilities* (Creamer 2009). In the book, Creamer presents a framework for thinking about disability. She frames disability as an unsurprising part of human limitations, to which all people are subject. Every human being has limitations; it is a condition that is common to all of us. If we think in terms of limitations, then we all have physical, mental, and emotional limitations. This is a very inclusive way of framing the question.

Perhaps in keeping with Creamer's approach is the idea that we all have limitations before the sovereign and providential God. Jeremiah's description of God's sovereignty and providence means that all persons are limited before God, but that our limitations do not prevent God from disciplining us, caring for our needs, or nurturing the divine/human relationship.

Importantly, as Rebecca Raphael acknowledges, the passages of Jeremiah that speak of people with disabilities, do not represent the voice of persons with disabilities. "Rather, we have the use of disability images by, about, and addressed to, an able-bodied audience" (Raphael 2011, 114). Her observation is crucial for assessing the book and its representation of disability. In the current chapter, we have been unable to access the living circumstances of real people with disabilities in ancient Judah. The book of Jeremiah does not include the voices or the social and cultural circumstances of people with disabilities.

As the passages of Jeremiah are interpreted, it is important to do what we can to reconstruct the lives of people with disabilities in the context of ancient Judah. Perhaps one way to increase our ability to do this is to listen carefully to the voices of persons with disability today. They may help biblical interpreters to know what to look for in these ancient texts. While it is true that this author has read numerous publications in disability studies, it is also important to communicate with people with disabilities directly and to read autobiographical texts, poetry, and other works created by individuals with disabilities.

3

"I Will Cleanse You from All Your Uncleanness"

The Book of Ezekiel

According to Ralph W. Klein, Ezekiel's "audience was to be 'Israel,' a holistic term in the book of Ezekiel, almost always referring to the entire people . . ." (Klein 1988, 16). This chapter will try to be attentive to any shifts in meaning for the term.

It is important to note that the impact on Jerusalem of the siege and subsequent exile was very significant, with devastating destruction of the city itself and severe impact on the psyche of Judah. This is well argued by D. L. Smith-Christopher (1997). Ezekiel was one of the elites in the city (as a member of the priesthood) who was taken into exile in Babylon in 597. Exile is both the circumstances in which the book of Ezekiel was written and the topical preoccupation of the book. This background is crucial to understanding the book.

·CHAPTERS 1–3

Interestingly, Daniel I. Block makes the comment about Ezekiel, "More than any other prophet, Ezekiel is a man possessed" (Block 1997, 89). Block makes this comment to illustrate how thoroughly Ezekiel is under the control of Yhwh, though it could also indicate the prophet's mental condition. Indeed, "the hand of Yhwh" may suggest how complete was the divine influence over Ezekiel (v. 3). Block suggests that the incomplete and confused nature of the Ezekiel's depiction of the vision in chapter 1 is due to Ezekiel's emotional state upon receiving the vision (Block 1997, 90–91): "In other words, the reason for the garbled and obscure shape of the account of the vision is to be found in the emotional state of the recipient, who by internal data is purported to have been the narrator of the experience as well" (Block 1997, 90–91).

In chapter 3, verses 7–9, the trait of obstinance is give a physical attribute:

> But the House of Israel will refuse to listen to you, for they refuse to listen to Me; for the whole House of Israel are hard of forehead and stubborn of heart. But I will make your face as hard as theirs, and your forehead as rigid as theirs. I will make your forehead like adamant, harder than flint. Do not fear them, and do not be dismayed by them, though they are a rebellious breed.

The physical description is meant to convey how unwilling the Israelites were to listen to the deity's commands (Block 2013, 5). The irony of the passage is that the people of other languages are prepared to listen, but the Israelites are not (Darr 1994, 1126). When moral failings are described by metaphors of the physical body, this can be problematic for people with disabilities. For too long, persons with disabilities have had others attribute moral failings to the disabled's physical condition.

After Ezekiel sees the presence of Yhwh in the plain, Yhwh informs Ezekiel that he should shut himself up in the house where he will be bound with cords so that he will be confined there. Thus, Ezekiel's ability to move about outside is restrained. Later in verses 26–27, the deity makes it impossible for Ezekiel to confront the exiles, to reprove them, because Yhwh had made Ezekiel's tongue "cleave to your palate." Ezekiel is rendered unable to speak at that point. However, when Yhwh wants Ezekiel to convey the deity's words to the people, Yhwh restores Ezekiel's ability to speak. Walther Zimmerli argues that these verses are more than metaphorical, reflecting real problems for Ezekiel (Zimmerli 1979, 160). These verses put Yhwh squarely in the driver's seat where speech is concerned. It is in the deity's hands to determine who speaks or who does not. This raises issues for people with disabilities who want to use the prophet Ezekiel for inspiration. To perceive the deity as someone who would dole out abilities related to the body is not helpful for developing a relationship with that deity. It is rather ironic that the prophet who sometimes cannot speak is charged with delivering a message to those who will not listen.

CHAPTERS 4–24

In chapter 4, verse 8, the deity restrains Ezekiel with cords until he completes his lengthy symbolic action signifying the sieges and exiles of both the Northern and Southern Kingdoms. Ezekiel is unable to turn from the right to the left or from left to the right, constrained by Yhwh. Of course, to a person with a disability that limits their mobility, the idea that the deity would limit someone's mobility is difficult to understand. Unfortunately, a person could make a connection between their own limited mobility and the will of Yhwh.

Later on, in chapter 5, the deity indicates that fully one-third of the Israelite population will die of pestilence or famine (v. 12). The sovereignty of God is stressed as Yhwh is represented as inflicting severe illness, starvation, and death as punishment for sin. As if pestilence (v. 17) was not enough, Yhwh also predicts that the people will be mocked by the surrounding nations (v. 14). Many people with disabilities have felt the sting of being mocked by others and it is unfortunate that it is connected with illness in this chapter.

Ezekiel 6:9 states: "Those of you who escape will remember me in the nations where they have been taken captive, how I was crushed by their adulterous heart that turned away from me and by their eyes which lusted after their idols; and they will loathe themselves in their own sight for the evils which they have done, for all their abominations." As Block points out, "remember" in this context implies a renewal of the divine-human relationship (Block 1997, 231). Scattered throughout the nations, the people will newly acknowledge Yhwh's sovereignty. In their self-loathing, they will be totally humbled before Yhwh and acknowledge their unworthiness before the divine (Block 1997, 232). The description of unfaithfulness in physical terms is not unusual for Ezekiel. Here the heart and eyes have betrayed the relationship with Yhwh. The dangers of such metaphors are obvious; to attribute moral failings to physical features is a practice that has made life difficult for many people with disabilities.

Part of the consequences of punishment is listed in chapter 7, verses 17–18. Once again, Ezekiel uses physical metaphors to indicate the depth of damage done by Yhwh's punishment: "All hands shall grow feeble, all knees will flow with water. They shall put on sackcloth; horror shall cover them. Shame shall be on all faces, baldness on all their heads" (vv. 17–18). Because of the overwhelming power of Yhwh's punishment, people will experience weak hands and urine will flow on their knees (see Block 1997, 261). The physical weakness is associated with shame as well as baldness! Katheryn Pfisterer Darr argues,

> In the face of such horrors, the people experience uncontrollable terror. Enfeebled hands are a physiological manifestation of psychological I anguish in the face of impending doom (Isa 13:7; Jer 50:43). The NRSV translation of v. 17b, 'all knees turn to water' (see also NIV), is misleading. The image refers to losing control of one's bladder. (Darr 1994, 1167)

Zimmerli suggests that the shame the people show in their faces reflect the deep humiliation and loss of honor that will come to them through the divine retribution (Zimmerli 1979, 208). The important point is that the fear that arose because of the deity's punishment was so overwhelming that it was manifested in physical ways. Shame was associated with the physical manifestations. The shame attributed to physical weakness is a difficult idea indeed when read through a disability lens.

More physical metaphors appear in Ezekiel 11:19–21, where Yhwh states that the people will have a singleness of heart; the people's stone heart will be substituted for a heart of flesh. This replacement will enable the people to follow the divine laws and rules. The substitution seems to be a prerequisite for the renewal of the covenant between Yhwh and the people (Block 1997, 352). Those who cling to their old hearts and their old ways will face the divine retribution. Of course, the idea that defective body parts can be replaced and that will solve all the problems of obedience is potentially offensive to people with disabilities. As Jason A. Staples points out, it is the exiles in Babylon who are regarded as the "preserved remnant" (Staples 2021, 136–37).

In chapter 12, verses 1–7, the deity describes rebellious people in metaphorical terms as those whose physical attributes exist, but they do not function: "O mortal, you dwell among the rebellious house. They have eyes to see but see not, ears to hear but hear not; for they are a rebellious house" (v. 2). Ironically, Ezekiel is told to engage in the symbolic act of leaving for exile "before their eyes" or "before their very eyes" (vv. 3–6). The attributes of seeing and hearing figure prominently in verses 2–6. Since the chapter predicts the exile, it reflects a period in Ezekiel's ministry before the fall of Jerusalem (Darr 1994, 1191). It portrays how disastrous and miserable the fall and exile would be. Of course, Ezekiel is reenacting something very painful from his own experience. However, the use of nonfunctional eyes and ears to portray rebellion is offensive to some persons with disabilities.

Chapter 14 employs physical metaphors quite frequently. For example, some elders of the house of Israel are described as having stumbled through their sin (vv. 3 and 4). To stumble because of sin draws upon a physical metaphor to describe wrongdoing and its consequences. The elders referenced here were likely representatives in the assembly (Kessler 2008, 125). Verse 4 further describes a person as "setting up idols in his heart," suggesting that the tendency to unfaithfulness and illicit worship reside in the body. By worshiping idols, the individual puts a "stumbling block in front of his face." Yʜwʜ questions whether it is appropriate for the deity to answer such a person's inquiry. The deity goes on to describe laying hold of people's hearts because of their estrangement (v. 4). In verse 6, Yʜwʜ commands these sinners to repent, to turn away from idols, and to turn their faces from their abominations. This verse uses metaphors that imply physical turning, including the admonition to repent. Some of the previous physical metaphors are repeated in verse 7. Yʜwʜ's response to this wrongdoing is given in verse 8: "I will set My face against that man and make him a sign and a byword, and I will cut him off from the midst of My people. Then you shall know that I am Yʜwʜ." Elsewhere in the Hebrew Bible, the phrase "set my face against" is sometimes associated with "I will cut him off" (Block 1997, 430; see also 15:7). This indicates that the deity's intention to punish the person is set, irrevocably, so that he will be cut off from the midst of his people. Yʜwʜ's intention is expressed by physical metaphor. The intention to punish is expressed by physical means again in verse 9: "I will stretch out my hand against him" (see also v. 13). Perhaps most pertinent to this study of disability in the Hebrew prophets, Yʜwʜ threatens famine (v. 13) and pestilence (v. 19) against those who sin. Ezekiel 15:7 suggests that "setting the face" then inflicting punishment will convince the people that Yʜwʜ is indeed God: "I will set My face against them; they escaped from fire, but fire shall consume them. When I set my face against them, you shall know that I am Yʜwʜ."

The association of transgressions or sins with physical features is problematic through the lens of disability. The deity's displeasure in chapter 14 is closely associated with the consequence of physical punishment. Many persons with disabilities have been subjected to theological theories that associate disability with punishment from the deity. In particular, the punishment of pestilence by the hand of Yʜwʜ suggests that chronic, serious illness could come from the hand of the deity. Anything other than the random occurrence of disability or chronic illness can be damaging emotionally to someone with a disability. It is also somewhat disturbing that it is through the intention and the action to punish that the people of Israel will know that Yʜwʜ is God.

CHAPTERS 25–32

In chapter 28, the attention turns from Yʜwʜ's discipline of Israel to Yʜwʜ's punishment of Tyre and Sidon. Thus, Ezekiel becomes a judge of the nations in this chapter and some following (Block 2013, 18). The siege of Tyre by Nebuchadnezzar likely started in 598 BCE and lasted for 13 years (Smith-Christopher 1997, 14). Yʜwʜ predicts that strangers will punish Tyre, that Tyre's claim to divinity will end in death, in drowning in the sea (vv. 7–8). Tyre is considered unclean and will suffer "the death of the uncircumcised" (v. 10). That should prove that to Tyre that its people are human, not divine. This is what Yʜwʜ does to cement the sovereignty that belongs to the deity. In mourning for the king of Tyre, Yʜwʜ extols his wisdom and flawless beauty (v. 12). Though at one time the king was physically flawless and morally upright, he has become corrupt through sin (v. 15). Yʜwʜ promises to destroy him. Block suggests that the idea of sin, then expulsion, has been derived from Genesis 3 (Block 1998, 116). Verse 17 gives the deity's reasons for this destruction: "Your heart was haughty because of your beauty, you corrupted your wisdom for the sake of your splendor; I have cast you to the ground, I have made you an object for kings to stare at." In this case, the king of Tyre's haughtiness is described as located in his heart. Because the king of Tyre's wisdom has become corrupted, Yʜwʜ will humiliate him. Another reason for the king's destruction is his dishonest dealing in trade. Through conflagration,

Tyre is destroyed (Block 1998, 117). As Block further notes, the oracle against the king of Tyre may also incorporate ancient Canaanite and Mesopotamian traditions (Block 1998, 119).

Ezekiel also conveys the word of God for Sidon. Through bloodshed and pestilence, the city of Sidon will be punished by Yhwh. Sidon's punishment will enable the deity to gain glory, be shown as holy, and communicate sovereignty to the people, that is, "They shall know that I am Yhwh." The outcome will also protect the Israelites from further harm from their neighbors. Sidon was part of an alliance against Babylon in 595/594 BCE. The king of Sidon is listed as a captive of Nebuchadrezzar's court, along with other representatives of nations (Darr 1994, 1398; see also Cogan 1999, 265).

According to Margaret S. Odell (Odell 2005, 372) as well as Karl S. Freedy and Donald B. Redford (Freedy and Redford 1970), the date formulae in Ezekiel's oracles against Egypt are accurate as much as scholars can determine about Egypt's activities at the time. Freedy and Redford use the date formulae to place the oracles against Egypt in their approximate historical context. For example, 29:1 is January/February 588/587 BCE, a full year after the beginning of the siege of Jerusalem; 30:20 is March/April 587, three months later; 31:1 is May/June 587; 29:17 is March/April is 571 BCE, the latest date in Ezekiel; 32:1 is thought to refer to March 586; while 32:17 is April 586 (Freedy and Redford 1970, 470–74). From Ezekiel's perspective, all takes place during the time Ezekiel is in Babylon.

When confronting Egypt with its misdeeds, Yhwh communicates divine sovereignty in no uncertain terms. Yhwh announces in chapter 29, verse 3: "I am going to deal with you, O Pharaoh, King of Egypt . . ." Ezekiel depicts Pharaoh as a monster crocodile, lurking in the Nile, stating: "My Nile is my own; I act for myself" (see Odell 2005, 373). Pharaoh is presented as arrogant, self-centered, and unreliable. Yhwh yanks Pharoah out of the Nile, with fish clinging to his scales. Then the divine sovereign flings the monster and the fish into the desert. Verse 6 compares Egypt's unreliability to a flimsy reed. Because Egypt failed to fulfill its promises to Judah, Yhwh will bring destruction to the country. Then, Egypt will know that Yhwh is God, not Pharoah. Nevertheless, as Odell points out, Egypt will eventually be restored to its original boundaries (Odell 2005, 372–73). As such, Egypt will no longer dominate other nations, nor will it entice Judah to trust Egypt as a reliable ally. Thus, this section intends to restore

Egypt to its proper size, as a country confined to its original boundaries and whose pharaoh no longer claims to be divine.

Some similar themes that we have seen earlier surface in Ezekiel 30, where the divine threat is directed toward Egypt. Like the passages about Tyre and Sidon, the divine punishment for Egypt has physical repercussions. Ezekiel 30:4 illustrates the nature of these metaphors, "A sword shall pierce Egypt, And Nubia shall be seized with trembling. When men fall slain in Egypt And her wealth is seized And her foundations are overthrown." Like other passages, fear produces shakiness (see also v. 9). Verse 6 indicates that Egypt's strength will be depleted, and she and her allies shall fall by the sword. In verse 8, the text predicts that Egypt will be destroyed by fire and anyone assisting her will be "broken." After these actions, the people will know that YHWH is sovereign.

Violent imagery becomes more specific and intense in verse 21, where YHWH indicates that he has broken Pharaoh's arm. The arm had not healed, nor had it had been bound up. Eventually, YHWH resolves to break the healthy arm of Pharaoh as well, so that he cannot use a sword. In contrast, YHWH will strengthen Nebuhadrezzar's arms (vv. 24–25). Then, the nations will know that he is the LORD (v. 26). This section of chapter 30 pictures the deity as causing severe injury to the king of Egypt, while the deity enhances the strength of the king of Babylon. The purpose is to show the deity's sovereignty over the nations, but it suggests as well that the deity causes injury, deciding who will be healthy and strong, and who shall deal with impairment. In light of the United States of America's involvement in foreign wars and the increased number of injured troops whose lives are spared, this depiction of YHWH is problematic.

CHAPTERS 33–39

Verse 10 stands out in chapter 33—"Now you, mortal, say to the house of Israel, 'Thus you have said: "Our transgressions and our sins weigh upon us, and we waste away because of them; how then can we live?"'"—because it suggests that wrongdoing can impact the Israelites physically. The verb translated as "waste away" is from the root מקק. In the Nifal the meaning of the verb is "to melt, dissolve" (Baumgartner and Koehler 2001, 629). Thus Ezekiel 33 describes the consequences of transgressing or sinning as the dissolving of the person. Nevertheless, the exiles did not perceive their experience in

Babylon after 597 as "a permanent residence, or even having ulti-mate meaning for them" (Sanders 1997, 53). This attitude is reflected in Ezekiel 33–34, 36–37.

It is not too much of a stretch to see behind this a theological point of view that associates deterioration of the body with sin-fulness. If a deteriorating condition is suspected to be the result of sinfulness, that is a theological concept that can impact people with disabilities in a negative way. These associations of illness, injury, or disability with sinfulness are one reason why an examination of scripture through the lens of disability can be important.

Chapter 34 is one of the most relevant sections in the book of Ezekiel for this study of disability in the Hebrew prophets. This chapter perhaps contains a direct reference to people with disabilities.

According to Block, the shepherds in Ezekiel 34 should be identified with the "former kings of Judah" (Block 1998, 282). In his argument, the first reason is that Ezekiel makes a clear distinc-tion between the shepherds and the sheep, even the sheep with power. "Second, according to vv. 23–24, the appointment of a sin-gle, good shepherd, David, who acts on behalf of the divine Shep-herd, represents the solution to the present problem of a series of bad shepherds" (Block 1998, 282). Several commentators agree that "shepherds" in Ezekiel 34 signify the former kings or rulers of Israel (see, e.g., Klein 1988, 121; Zimmerli 1983, 213). However, Ralph W. Klein suggests that the term "shepherds" may include the current leaders of the community in exile, with a focus on the former kings (Klein 1988, 121). Nevertheless, as Block acknowledges, the primary focus is on the flock (Klein 1988, 283). "The leaders are introduced mainly because their actions have precipitated the crisis and cre-ated the need for divine intervention on behalf of the sheep" (Klein 1988, 283). Among the worst crimes of the bad shepherds were their lack of concern for the physical health of the sheep, their failure to strengthen the weak, to heal the sick, or bind up the injured (Klein 1988, 284; Ezekiel 34:4). According to Rainer Kessler, "the parable of the shepherd (Ezekiel 34) is also based on contrasts between shep-herds and flocks (rulers and people), as well as between the strong and weak in the flock itself" (Kessler 2008, 131).

Verse 2 accuses the leaders of Israel of having benefitted them-selves when they should have been shepherding the sheep. Ezekiel 34 claims that the leaders have some responsibilities for the people that they govern. They should be providing for the sheep, making sure that they eat well. In this extended metaphor, Ezekiel accuses the leaders of ingesting the milk, wearing the wool, and eating the meat of the sheep, but these same leaders have not fed the sheep (v. 3). Verse 4 gets specific about what the leaders have neglected to do: they have failed to strengthen the weak, nor have they healed the sick. The injured (broken) were not bound up, those driven away were not brought back, and the leaders did not seek for those who were lost. At the end of verse 4, the leaders are accused of ruling over the sheep with force and cruelty.

Verse 5 of chapter 34 suggests that the flock has been neglected as they have been scattered over the face of the earth, with no one searching for them or seeking them. Because they had no shepherd—that is, the leaders made no effort to protect the people—the people were vulnerable and thus they were scattered widely. This is a very clear reference to the Babylonian Exile, reflecting a time after some Judahites were removed from their homeland and taken to Babylonian territory. (Given the reference in 33:21, "in the twelfth year of our exile," this likely refers to 585 BCE.) This passage places the culpability for the exile squarely in the hands of the leadership. Because they were not responsible for the people and did not tend to their needs, the exile and scattering of the people was an inevitable consequence.

In the following verses, 7–10, the passage presents YHWH's words as directly confronting Israel's leadership, reiterating their crimes against the people. In answer to this, YHWH intends to remove the elites from their positions of leadership. It will no longer be possible for the shepherds to profit from the sheep, for YHWH will remove the sheep from "their hand" (v. 9).

Finally, YHWH promises to be the good shepherd, to take over the duties of the earthly shepherds and become the good shepherd that the sheep deserve. Most relevant for the task at hand, YHWH promises to do the things that the earthly shepherds failed to do: YHWH will feed the sheep, seek the lost, bring back those driven away, bind up the injured, and heal the sick.

This passage has direct relevance for people with disabilities. Ezekiel 34 makes the case that those who govern have responsibilities toward those who are infirm, marginalized, or excluded from the community.

Yhwh's sovereignty is upheld by the chapter. It is Yhwh who reserves the right to judge in righteousness. Through this judgment process, Yhwh takes to task the leadership who drinks from clean water, but then muddies it for those who follow.

In addressing the mountains of Israel, verse 15 states that yhwh will prevent the land from causing the nations within it to stumble. Again, Ezekiel depicts sinfulness in physical terms. The linkage between wrongdoing and physical issues can be problematic for people with disabilities.

This chapter envisions the future restoration of Israel. The entire passage is mostly positive in tone and intent. An exception occurs in verse 17: "O mortal, when the House of Israel dwelt on their own soil, they defiled it with their ways and their deeds; their ways were in My sight like the uncleanness of a menstruous woman." In the attempt to explain the destruction of the Southern Kingdom and the exile of much of the population, Ezekiel describes their wrongdoing and how it defiled the land. However, the passage compares the defilement of the land to "the uncleanness of a menstruous woman." This denigrates a healthy, natural process that women undergo. It is unfair to characterize a natural process as defiling. This has implications for people with disabilities when their bodies are perceived in similar ways.

Later in the chapter, Yhwh takes responsibility for the scattering of the people to other lands. Yhwh also blames the exiles for defiling Yhwh's holy name. Again, defilement or uncleanness is associated with transgressions by the people. So, those who have sinned become ritually unclean, with implications for bodies that are unclean by insinuation. People with disabilities have long been burdened by thoughts that they must have done something to bring their disabilities on.

Of course, verses 24–28 portray Yhwh as promising to gather all the people back to the land of Israel. According to Staples, these verses envision the reuniting of both Israel and Judah (Staples 2021, 136). In addition, Yhwh intends to cleanse the people of their impurities:

> I will take you from among the nations and gather you from all the countries, and I will bring you back to your own land. I will sprinkle clean water upon you, and you shall be clean: I will

cleanse you from all your uncleanness and from all your fetishes. And I will give you a new heart and put a new spirit into you: I will remove the heart of stone from your body and give you a heart of flesh; and I will put My spirit into you. Thus, I will cause you to follow My laws and faithfully to observe My rules. Then you shall dwell in the land which I gave to your fathers, and you shall be My people and I will be your God.

Though the language used in this passage should be understood as metaphorical, to remove a person's heart and replace it with a new heart does imply an easy fix for a physical problem. Many people with disabilities live with the knowledge that there is no physical solution for their disabilities. The removal of the stone heart also suggests that any body part that does not function well can be easily removed.

One might consider the chapter on dry bones as representing disability at the end of the spectrum, as the most extreme example of disability. In the passage, Ezekiel is transported by the spirit to view the dry bones in a valley. He is brought into the midst of the bones and told to prophesy to them. The bones are described as "very dry" (v. 2) to heighten the sense of the healing action brought about through Ezekiel's prophesy. When Ezekiel prophesies to the dry bones, they came together, bone to bone. Then sinews come upon them, flesh covers them, then skin comes over that. As Ezekiel continues to prophesy breath comes into them and they live!

Though the action of God is inspiring and wonderful to behold, according to chapter 37, there remains a problem from the perspective of disability. Many people who have disabilities do not experience physical healing. Certainly, no disability is as extreme as death, yet the question remains: if God has the power to bring the dry bones to life, why are some persons with disability left without healing? While the purpose of the passage may be to illustrate God's extraordinary healing power, does it make that illustration at the expense of persons with disabilities?

Another purpose for the vision of dry bones, understood from its historical context, is to convince the exiles in Babylon that there is life for the children of Israel after all. Like the dry bones, Israel will experience renewal, "shall live again." Specifically, verse 11 states that "the bones are the whole house of Israel." Continuing with the extended metaphor of bringing life to the dead, God promises to bring the Israelites out of their graves and restore them to their land.

Verse 22 states that both of the scattered kingdoms—Northern and Southern Kingdoms—will be restored to the land and form one nation restored to the land. Indeed, all the people of Israel will be cleansed of their sin through God's actions. Once cleansed, the children of Israel will again be God's people and YHWH would be their God. Finally, God establishes a new covenant of peace with the children of Israel.

The passage makes the case for Israel's restoration to the land as the people of God. This case is made very effectively. Nevertheless, the extended metaphor of the dry bones brought back to life creates some tensions for modern day readers. Readers may ask why the divine power to restore cannot be applied by persons with disabilities. Why isn't this divine power available to all who may benefit from it?

THEOLOGICAL IMPLICATIONS

An important physical motif in Ezekiel, that is, "to stumble," is worthy of analysis. The noun מִכְשׁוֹל means "something on which one stumbles, hindrance, offence" (Baumgartner and Koehler 2001, 582). This form occurs in Ezekiel 3:20, 7:19, 14:3–7, 18:30, and 44:12. The verbal root כשל arises numerous times in Ezekiel as well: Ezekiel 33:12 (nif.); 36:14 (pi.); 36:15 (hif.); and 21:20 (hof.). The meaning of "to stumble" (nif.) is consistent with "cause to stumble, stagger" (hof.). The motif of stumbling is associated with transgressions. Either the people of Israel have created a stumbling block due to their sinning or YHWH has put a stumbling block in front of the people because of their wrongdoing (for example, in 18:30, YHWH threatens to put a "stumbling block of iniquity" before those who transgress). Often the trouble is with the worship of idols. However, to make the point about wrongdoing, Ezekiel uses the metaphor of stumbling to illustrate the consequences of sinning, consequences exacted by YHWH.

One issue raised by a reading of the book of Ezekiel is the attribution of obstinance or disobedience to physical traits. In chapter 3, for instance, Ezekiel refers to being "hard of forehead" and "stubborn of heart." Chapter 6 refers to "adulterous hearts" and "eyes that lust after idols." In chapter 11 YHWH indicates that the people's stone hearts will be replaced with a heart of flesh. Verses 1–7 in chapter 12 focus on non-functional body parts—eyes and ears—to indicate the rebellious nature of the people of Judah. They have eyes but cannot see; ears but cannot hear. This metaphor of the stone heart occurs again in Ezekiel 36. The purpose of these metaphors is to make the issues with Judah's (and Israel's) behaviors vivid to the readers/listeners. However, to attribute wrongdoing and sinfulness to physical features can be off-putting to readers or listeners.

Also in chapter 3, YHWH restrains Ezekiel physically with cords in his home and takes away his ability to speak. Eventually, YHWH restores Ezekiel's power of speech and instructs Ezekiel about what to say. In chapter 4, Ezekiel is bound by chords by YHWH until he is ready to perform a symbolic action. The picture of YHWH as a powerful God who would physically restrain a prophet is disturbing. Rather than persuading the prophet to represent YHWH, the deity "strong arms" Ezekiel into serving as prophet. This use of power is difficult to see. It does raise the question of freedom of choice. Can the prophet say no?

A concern that surfaces in reading Ezekiel is the idea that people will come to know YHWH through severe punishment: through famine, pestilence, fire, or death by violence. These acts are intended to make the people turn back to YHWH. I wonder if that is an effective means to attract people to worship the divine. While the book encourages people to adhere to the social justice aspects of the covenant, reflecting concern for the neighbor, widow, and orphan, the means of enforcing the covenant are very severe and sometimes disabling. To portray the deity as inflicting disability or death on the people in order to ensure obedience to the covenant is disturbing when read through a disability lens. One way of making YHWH's sovereignty known is using the deity's awesome power to crush any nation which oppresses Judah. See, for example, YHWH's treatment of Pharaoh in Ezekiel 29. After Pharaoh is cast into the wilderness to serve as food for the wild animals and birds, "the inhabitants of Egypt will know that I am YHWH." Once again, the divine sovereignty is made known and people come to know the divine through excruciating punishment. Of course, chapter 30 reflects YHWH breaking Pharaoh's arms and strengthening the arms of Babylon's king.

In contrast to what we have discerned about YHWH from previous chapters, Ezekiel 34 presents YHWH as the good shepherd, as someone who will care for the weak, the sick, and the injured. YHWH takes the leaders of Judah to task for failing to protect and nurture the people. In this chapter, very positively for our study, YHWH shows a particular concern for those who are physically challenged, whether it is through weakness, illness, or injury. This is a much more favorable image of the deity as one who will gently care for the sheep as a "good shepherd" would.

Ezekiel 36 makes the case that the people's sins have defiled the land. However, YHWH promises to gather the people back to the land (presumably from exile in other lands) and cleanse them from their impurities. In this way, the deity will remove the effects of their sin and return the people, purified for life in their homeland. This is an encouraging representation of YHWH, one that illustrates the salvation that comes from God. YHWH will welcome the people back from exile and will ready them for ritual service by cleansing them from any defilement. To keep the people on the right track, YHWH will also prepare them spiritually by removing their heart of stone and replacing it with a new heart.

4

"Assemble the Lame and Outcast"
The Book of the Twelve

HOSEA

It is likely that the prophetic oracles in the book of Hosea were written in the historical context of the mid- and later eighth century BCE (Dearman 2010, 3). Robin Routledge places the date more precisely, claiming that most of the material in Hosea dates to 725 BCE, at a time when Assyria was a potent threat, but before the fall of the Northern Kingdom in 722/21 (Routledge 2020, 2). J. Andrew Dearman suggests that Hosea's prophetic ministry may have lasted thirty years (Dearman 2010, 78). "This long time span is suggested by the contents of the book, which alludes to the 'sin of Jezreel' yet to be punished, along with references to Israel's political entanglements with Egypt and Assyria (Hos 1:4–5; 5:13–14; 7:11–13; 8:8–10; 9:5–6; 11:10–11; 14:3)" (Miller and Hayes 2006, 359).

Important to our task here is the use of rhetorical analysis, especially in the study of metaphors, as Brad E. Kelle describes it: "The metaphors, it is argued, are not merely decorative devices, but function as part of the intended communication designed to reshape the thinking and behavior of a particular audience in a specific rhetorical context. Such analysis allows an interpreter to move beyond historical concerns and offer a rhetorical critique of the metaphors in a book like Hosea, exposing how they work rhetorically to construct certain understandings of reality . . ." (Kelle 2010, 324).

Hosea 4–14

As we move into the latter section of Hosea, chapter 4 has some pertinent passages for our task. In chapter 4, YHWH has a case to bring against Israel, a case that focuses on the people of the land's sinful behavior. Because of that behavior, "the land mourns: Everything that dwells on it withers away" (v. 3a). As Hans Walter Wolff points out, the root אמל means withered vegetation primarily but it is also used to signify childlessness (Wolff 1974, 68). Thus, the land will be destroyed, without the ability to support life. Birds, beasts of the field, and fish will succumb. Though not mentioned specifically, human beings will perish as well. As they face the consequences of their actions, the priest will stumble by day and a prophet will stumble by night (v. 5). The metaphor of stumbling is used to convey the fall of Israel through the priest's and prophet's moral failure. The people of the land will suffer consequences because of the sinfulness of their leaders (vv. 6–7).

This representation of "stumbling" tends to equate mobility impairment with sinful behavior. The ability to ambulate without stumbling or falling is made equivalent to moral uprightness. These metaphors can be harmful to those with disabilities. To see issues of mobility as the consequence of sin can create painful attitudes toward people with physical disabilities.

The chapter goes on to say that the people are destroyed for want of knowledge, the priest is rejected because of forgetting YHWH's instruction, so YHWH will forget the children of Israel (v. 6). In this context, the lack of knowledge means the failure to know God (Mays 1969, 69). Thus, the verse is not taking issue with people who lack general knowledge or who have an intellectual disability. Rather, the concern is with knowledge of God and obedience to the Torah. These are the reasons given for the impending catastrophe. As James Luther Mays describes it, "'knowledge' is learning and obeying the will of the covenant of God in devotion and faithfulness . . ." (Mays 1969, 69). The implication is that the priest has not done his covenantal duty, which entails adhering to and teaching others about the deity's instructions (Wolff 1974, 79). The theme of stumbling appears again in verse 14; because of the people's lechery and promiscuousness they will stumble (that is, their nation will fall).

In chapter 5, the listeners are encouraged rhetorically to be attentive to the message by appealing to the physical. They are exhorted to hear (שׁמעו), to attend (והקשׁיבו), and to give ear (האזינו). The last term comes from a verbal root that also generates the noun meaning "ear" (אֹזֶן). The exhortation to the priests and the royal house to listen is construed in physical terms, that is, "to give ear." They are told that right conduct is the responsibility of those in leadership. Later, in verse 3, Israel is described as "defiled" (נטמא). Though "defiled" is used metaphorically here, it does refer at its root to a physical state of uncleanness. Indeed, Israel's habits have prevented a turning back to God (v. 4). Devotion and faithfulness to God are expressed through physical metaphor as a "turning" (לָשׁוּב) to God. Because of the spirit of idolatry, the people of Israel do not know God. Verse 5 continues with physical metaphors as Israel, Ephraim, and Judah shall stumble through their iniquity.

Finally, chapter 5 depicts Ephraim as sick, Judah as having sores. The sickness causes the people to turn to Assyria for assistance. The passage in verse 13 reminds the reader that Assyria will not be able to cure illness nor heal wounds. Yet, though Israel is terribly ill, Yhwh refuses to offer help. Instead, the deity intends to return to his abode. The implication is that Yhwh has the power to heal Ephraim and Judah but refuses to do so because of their unfaithfulness. They turn to Assyria for help and not to God. Dearman outlines what Yhwh's healing would look like in this situation: "In this instance YHWH's cure would mean removing Israel's dependence on other deities and the power of Assyria, restoring them to fidelity and sole dependence on him, and then granting them the blessings promised in the covenant" (Dearman 2010, 186).

Many people with disabilities have experienced disappointment that God does not provide healing. Yet, in these verses, God refuses to heal, though having the power to restore to health and wholeness. It is problematic to portray the deity in this fashion as attacking like a lion (v. 14) rather than helping those who are ill or injured. This contributes to people with disabilities feeling alienated from religious institutions. The passage also attributes the infirmities to sinfulness on the part of Ephraim and Judah. This use of the metaphor of illness and injury helps shape a tendency on the part of readers to attribute disability to wrongdoing.

The beginning of chapter 6 opens with a voice that persuades listeners (readers) to become obedient to Yнwн. The reasoning is that since God had attacked, then God can heal. Since God is the one who wounds, then God will be the one who binds those wounds. The voice argues that God can make the people whole (6:2): "He will revive us after two days. On the third day, he will raise us up that we may live before him." The deity responds by stating that steadfast love (חסד) is more important than sacrifice and knowledge of God more important than burnt offerings. In verse 7, we read: "They, as at Adam, transgressed the covenant [Dearman 2010, 188]. There they dealt treacherously with me."

Another verse of interest to our project is chapter 7, verse 5: "On the day of our king the officials became sick with the heat of wine; he stretched out his hand with mockers" (NRSV). The next two verses, 6–7, present a picture of people fired up like ovens; their anger is enflamed every morning. They have destroyed their judges and the kings have fallen. This is a depiction of political intrigue which has consumed the Northern Kingdom. The people are sick from drunkenness. Their own fury keeps them agitated and the Kingdom is falling to ruin. More physical metaphors are used later in chapter 7, specifically in verses 8–11. Ephraim is described as mixing himself among the peoples and he is like a cake that has not been turned (that is, flipped over; v. 8). This may refer to Israel's switching of allegiances from Egypt and Aram to Assyria (Wolff 1974, 125–26). The cake metaphor may suggest that Ephraim was incapable of turning back to Yнwн. Foreigners have consumed his strength, but he does not know it. Grey hairs are scattered upon his head, but he does not know it (v. 9). Circumstances have aged Israel and his strength has faded. Though Israel has been humbled before his very eyes, the people have not seen fit to turn back to Yнwн (v. 10). Verse 11 concludes by saying that Ephraim has acted like a silly dove, turning this way toward Egypt, and that way toward Assyria. Verse 13 confirms Yнwн's stance that Ephraim had strayed from him and reaffirmed the intention to destroy them. The chapter ends with the voice of Yнwн claiming to have braced and strengthened the Israelites' arms, yet the people plan evil against Yнwн. The people have turned back to God, but the voice of the deity complains that they are largely useless, like a slack bow. The voice predicts that officials would fall by the sword because of their stammering and babbling in the land of Egypt (see JPS translation, vv. 15–16).

All this physical description leads the reader to perceive Israel as corrupt and doomed to fall. One physical metaphor after another draws a vivid picture of Israel's faithlessness and their failure to return to God. Their punishment will be violent and will bring the nation to ruin. These depictions are designed to explain the destruction that will befall Israel through the Assyrians. The imagery of weakness, sickness, and Israel's ineffectuality make graphic their deceitfulness toward Yhwh. This language is rhetorically effective, but it also shapes the reader's understanding of physical weakness, sickness, and injury as associated with moral failing.

Two things of particular interest occur in chapter 9. First, there is a reference to the prophet being driven mad by harassment in the house of God (v. 7). Second, there is the appeal to God, presumably from the prophet, to make the people infertile (vv. 14–16), or if children are born to them that the children do not live to adulthood (v. 16).

Chapter 11 promises punishment for turning to Assyria and Egypt instead of Yhwh and because of the people's refusal to repent. In verse 6, the sword surges through the cities of Israel and devours their bones because of their schemes. As Wolff suggests, this may reflect the impending situation of Shalmaneser V and his troops as they slash their way through Israel beginning in 733 BCE (Wolff 1974, 200). Though presented with the specter of war, the people of Israel do not return to God; they do not respond when called upward (v. 7). In the United States of America, after decades of war in Iraq and Afghanistan, people understand the damage that war can do. These wars have created many people with disabilities resulting from injury. The close of chapter 11 shows Yhwh experiencing a change of heart, unable to give Ephraim up.

Chapter 13 reflects the internal struggle Yhwh has faced when the people of Israel have been unfaithful. On the one hand, Yhwh has cared for the people in the desert (v. 5), but on the other hand, Yhwh intends to discipline the people with violence because they have strayed: "Like a bear deprived of her young, I attack them; and rip open the covering of their hearts. I will devour them there like a lion. The beasts of the field shall mangle them." Verses 12 and 13 continue the theme of Ephraim's sin against Yhwh. Ephraim's sin is bound up and kept in store, meaning that he is unwilling to give it up (v. 12). In verse 13, metaphors of childbirth are used to indicate that Ephraim is experiencing pain, but he is unwilling to experience the new life that YHWH is offering. The verse describes the pains of childbirth coming for Ephraim, but he is "an unwise son" who does not present himself at the appropriate time in the birth canal.

To describe the birth experience as somehow remiss, is effective in serving as a wakeup call for Hosea's audience, but the association of unfaithfulness with the birth process is problematic for those for whom that has been a difficult experience.

Of course, 14:1 repeats the theme of infants and pregnant women as YHWH threatens to dash infants against the rocks and to rip open pregnant women. According to this verse, Samarians deserve such treatment because of their sinfulness.

JOEL

Joel is an intriguing and inspiring prophetic book, likely from the era of the Persian empire's dominance. However, it does not contain much of interest for the task at hand, so we will move on to Amos.

AMOS

Based on data reflected in the book of Amos, a significant earthquake and a possible eclipse in Amos 8:9, most scholars suggest that Amos' prophetic ministry occurred around 760 BCE (Carroll 2020, 6–7). Though the book of Amos does not explicitly mention the Assyrian Empire, it expanded and grew more powerful after the ascension of Tiglath-Pileser III to the throne in 745 BCE. His influential campaigns in Syria-Palestine lie in the background of the book (see Carroll 2020, 8); at least the threat of the Assyrian presence loomed large in Israelite politics of the time. Nevertheless, the lack of specificity for Assyria in the book and the absence of any references to governmental policy change to accommodate the empire, suggest a *terminus ad quem* of ca. 750 BCE for Amos' prophetic activity, as M. Daniel Carroll R. suggests (Carroll 2020, 9).

Much of the book's focus is on socioeconomic inequities. The Northern Kingdom, Israel, was experiencing a time of relative prosperity, but, according to the book, the nation was steeped in self-delusion about their circumstances. However, archaeological and epigraphical evidence supports the impression conveyed by the biblical text of Amos, with a level of social stratification (Carroll 2020, 15–16). At times in the reign of Jeroboam II there was relative peace and Israel could trade its agricultural products internationally, but as Aram and Assyria gained in power and influence the government would have raised taxes to provide for national defenses. This would put the agricultural workers, the predominant section of society, at a disadvantage. This was the group that was, by and large, barely making a living on the land. Adding a tax burden on top of that would make things more precarious for this group.

At any rate, Amos often condemns the wealthy who take advantage of the poor. This is very relevant to the project at hand because people with disabilities, according to the National Council on Disability, are more than twice as likely to live in poverty than the general population. "People with disabilities make up approximately 12 percent of the U.S. working-age population; however, they account for more than half of those living in long-term poverty. The median annual income for households receiving federal rental assistance from the three primary HUD programs is $13,500" (National Council on Disability 2017). Thus, issues of poverty and income disparity are very germane to our study.

In the oracles against the nations, Amos takes issue with Israel's treatment of the poor: "For three transgressions of Israel and for four, I will not revoke the punishment because they sell the righteous for silver and the needy for a pair of sandals. They who trample the head of the poor into the dust of the ground; and pervert the way of the afflicted" (2:6–7a). Similarly, in chapter 4, verse 1, the elite women of Bashan are accused of oppressing the poor and crushing the needy. They carouse to excess. Amos 5:11 states: "Therefore because you trample the poor and you take from them levies of grain." The following verse accuses the Israelites of subverting the cause of the needy in the gate. Other passages indicate that the elite status of the wealthy may indeed be turned on its head. Amos 8:4–6 again addresses the situation of the poor, admonishing the Israelites for devouring the needy and annihilating the poor. Verse 6 again employs the motif of the buying the poor for silver and the needy for a pair of sandals.

To a significant degree, the punishment of Israel, according to the book of Amos, is due to the people's treatment of the poor and needy. Certainly, socioeconomic matters are central to the book's concerns. Of course, the book also refers in more general terms to the Israelites' failure to adhere to standards of righteousness and justice (Amos 5:7; 5:15, 24; 6:12).

Punishment of Israel or other nations is conceived primarily in physical terms in Amos. Lest the Israelites think that they are too strong to be affected by Yhwh's punishment, Amos 2:9 makes the case that the Amorites were very strong and tall like a robust tree, but Yhwh was able to thoroughly destroy the Amorites. In verses 13 and 14, human limits in the face of the deity's power are explored: God will slow them down, despite their swiftness; the strong will become weak, and the warrior will not be able to save a life. Verses 15 and 16 develop the idea that God has sovereignty over the fate of all people, no matter who they are or how strong.

The physical nature of divine punishment is emphasized in 4:6 where Yhwh complains that the people did not return to him even after he caused famine in the land and drought in 4:8. In verse 10, the divinely caused pestilence is mentioned, yet the people did not return to Yhwh. At the close of chapter 4, the reader is reminded of God's sovereignty because of the creative power cited here.

Amos 5 predicts that Israel will fall and begins to intone a dirge over the nation (vv. 1–2). Verse 9 reminds the reader of God's creative power. Chapter 8 repeats some of the same themes: the fall of Israel, the mourning of the people, the reversal of creation (like the darkening of the sun), famine in the land, and thirst. In the beginning of chapter 9, Amos indicates that the people will perish by the sword. Yet, in the last section, verses 13–16, Yhwh promises to restore Israel fully, with abundant harvests, a return to the soil, rebuilt homes, vineyards, and gardens.

Focusing on the physical nature of Yhwh's punishment illustrates divine sovereignty over all things physical for human beings. God is in control, insisting upon people's faithfulness to the Divine One. The book of Amos makes it clear that no matter how wealthy, powerful, or physically strong a person is, Yhwh can exert the divine will over them.

OBADIAH

Obadiah does not contain much for the task at hand, so we will move on to Micah.

JONAH

Jonah does not contain much for the task at hand, so we will move on to Micah.

MICAH

The scholarly consensus about Micah the prophet places his prophetic career between a time before the destruction of the Northern Kingdom in 722 BCE and 701 BCE, the time of Sennacherib's invasion of Jerusalem (Simundson 1996, 534). Many scholars suggest that Micah's prophetic ministry started in the 730s. "Most scholars have associated his threats to the city of Jerusalem with Sennacherib's invasion in 701 BCE, although a minority would confine his career to a shorter span, ending perhaps within a decade after it had begun" (Simundson 1996, 534). Of course, the threat and reality of Neo-Assyrian oppression has been part of the horizon for Israel in the time of Micah after the Western campaign of Tiglath-Pileser III and his successors (Smith-Christopher 2015, 9). Of course, the political instability in the Northern Kingdom at this time contributed to the conflicts and inequities that existed. The opening chapter of Micah reflects the political tensions that surfaced with the Syro-Phoenician War. Not all the inhabitants of Judah were in support of Ahaz, but rather would have liked to see Judah join the anti-Assyrian coalition (Miller and Hayes 2006, 395).

The first passage of interest to us is Micah 1:8–9: "Because of this, I will wail and howl; I will go stripped and naked. I will make a wailing like the jackals and mourn like the ostriches. For her wound is incurable, it has reached Judah. It has spread to the gate of my people, to Jerusalem." This reference to an incurable wound is very pertinent to our task. The voice is likely to be that of God. In this context, it may very well be that YHWH is experiencing the pathos that the divine may feel in the prophets. As Daniel L. Smith-Christopher states: "What is involved in this destruction—however angrily Micah may have delivered the judgment—is also cause for sadness over the suffering involved" (Smith-Christopher 2015, 63). This author differs from me in perceiving Micah's personal voice in this, but the sadness at seeing the suffering of the Israelites is certainly the meaning intended.

In speaking about the impending punishment, chapter 2, verse 3 reminds the reader of the Israelites' tendency to plot evil, to seize others' property, etc. YHWH intends to bring such misfortune that the Israelites will not be able to remove their necks from it. In fact, things will be so bad that the people will not be able to walk erect. This punishment is conceived in physical terms. The people will have their mobility impaired. Though God has compassion for the people's suffering according to one passage, God will cause the people to be unable to walk upright in another. It is difficult to reconcile the punishing God with the one who feels deep sympathy for the people.

In a very graphic way, Micah 3:3 envisions how cruel the rulers have been to their people, reciting the deeds of the leaders of both Israel and Judah. This is described as devouring the people's flesh, flailing their skin, and breaking their bones. The verse uses graphic physical metaphors to illustrate how very pitiless and harsh the leaders have been to their people. Using these means brings home vividly how deserving of punishment the leadership is. The shock value of these explicit depictions is designed to convince readers of how complicit the rulers have been in leading the people astray. However, to a person in my historical context these are severe, violent illustrations.

Chapter 3, verses 5–7 take the prophets to task for falsely prophesying "peace." However, YHWH will bring darkness so that the prophets cannot prophesy; and the seers will be unable to see to offer their observations. They will experience shame because they receive no response from God. In these instances, God will change the physical elements so that the prophets may not function in their usual tasks.

Micah 4 conveys a vision of restoration, one in which the temple becomes prominent and the nations stream to it in order to gain knowledge of YHWH. In the literary context of this vision of restoration, YHWH promises to "assemble the lame and the outcast" as well as gather the people whom YHWH has afflicted (v. 6). The divine promise goes further to assure that "the lame" will become a remnant and the outcast a strong nation (v. 7). While the parallel of "the lame" with the outcast is troubling, this is a vision of inclusion. Instead of the person with a mobility disability being confined to the margins, this vision moves the individuals with disabilities to the center when YHWH rebuilds the nation. Later, in verse 13, the people are to receive a horn of iron and hooves of bronze to enable them to crush other nations. What is left of these nations' wealth will be dedicated to Yʜwʜ.

As a response to the restoration of God's people, in Micah 7:16 the nations will see and be ashamed, put their hands over their mouths, and "their ears shall be deaf." According to J. Blake Couey, "similar bodily reactions are depicted in the Hebrew Bible as natural responses to overwhelming experiences . . ." (Couey 2017, 253). In the case of Micah 7:16, the deity renders the nations deaf. The deity is portrayed as responsible for loss of hearing among the peoples. Of course, placing the inclination to disable in the hands of God is disturbing, but it is used here to indicate the nations in shock and awe as they come to know the God of Israel. Theologically, this is disturbing, to think that God would deliberately disable someone to make a point. In this case, the nations seem to come to a better understanding of who God is. Verse 17 depicts the nations trembling with fear before God.

NAHUM

The scholarly consensus places the historical prophet Nahum as engaging in prophetic ministry sometime between 663 BCE (shortly after the fall of Thebes to Ashurbanipal) and 612 (the fall of Ninevah, Assyria's capital). The fall of Thebes is described in Nahum 3:8 (Christiensen 2009, 54). The destruction of Ninevah is described in a compelling way. Though it had been a peaceful place, that peace is violently disrupted as indicated in verse 11, where the city is described as empty, desolate, and waste. Hearts melt and knees shake; loins quiver; and all faces grow pale. The devastation of Ninevah is portrayed in physical terms. The fear of the populace is conveyed by means of physical metaphor. As the siege of the city progresses, Nahum describes the numerous corpses in the streets (Nahum 3:3). The impending devastation is described by Yʜwʜ like the public humiliation of an adulteress, where her skirts are lifted high above her head so that all can see her nakedness (v. 5). The passage conveys the shame that comes with the defeat of a formerly great city. Verse 6 continues: "I will cast filth upon you, treat you with contempt, and make you a spectacle." The shame of the city will be physically evident because of God's punishing action against Ninevah. As the city goes into exile, her babies are dashed to pieces at the street corner (v. 10). Nahum 3:19 closes the book by declaring

Ninevah's wound grievous as well as incurable. To add to the pain, the nations are portrayed as clapping with joy over Assyria's defeat.

HABAKKUK

One aspect of Habakkuk that makes the book appealing for our particular task is its focus on justice (on Hababbuk's central concern with justice, see Hiebert 1996, 623–24). According to Theodore Hiebert, "the challenge of believing in the ultimate power of justice in a world that appears to be overwhelmingly unjust is one of the most difficult existential struggles the religious person must face. Among biblical writers, Habakkuk was not alone in wrestling with it" (Hiebert 1996, 624). In this multifaceted approach to disability in the book of Habakkuk, the concern for social justice is very important, so we will pursue the topic to an extent here.

It is difficult—on the basis of evidence within the book—to establish a time frame for Habakkuk's prophetic ministry. Unlike several of the prophetic books, the superscription does not offer a list of kings whose reigns overlap Habakkuk's career. However, the book does mention the Chaldeans in 1:6 and that aids in establishing a historical context (Hiebert 1996, 625). "Chaldean" is the biblical term used to describe the Neo-Babylonians who became a major power under Nabopolassar (626–605 BCE). Habukkuk predicted the invasion of Judah by the Neo-Babylonians, which happened first in 597 (Hiebert 1996, 626). Hiebert suggests that "Habukkuk's announcement of the Chaldean invasion was delivered between these events, in 605–604 BCE, the fifth year of the reign of Jehoaikim, king of Judah . . ." (Hiebert 1996, 626). In other words, Habukkuk predicted the Chaldean invasion after the Babylonians defeated the Assyrians and Egyptians at Carchemish in 605.

From the beginning of the book, Habakkuk is concerned about justice. He expresses his internal conflict caused by looking on injustice, waiting for action to restore justice, and seeing the apparent success of the wicked. In answer, Yhwh promises to raise of the Chaldeans, to confront the people of Judah with their unrighteousness, as divine punishment for wickedness (1:6–11). Verses 12 and 13 acknowledge in Habukkuk's voice that God is eternal and loathe to look on evil and wrongdoing.

An answer of sorts is provided in chapter 2, verses 2–4. In this section, reflecting yhwh's voice, the answer states that Habakkuk should write down the vision or revelation that he receives so that "a herald may run with it" (NIV, v. 2b). The deity reassures the prophet that a vision will come, though it may seem to be delayed, it will surely come. This message will indicate an end, a time when the observed inconsistencies and injustices will cease. It communicates reliably, honestly. Habakkuk was instructed to wait for the vision/message. The prophet is reminded that the spirit of the proud is not right within them, "but the righteous will live by their faith" (v. 4b). Though the latter phrase has been quite significant in Protestantism in the doctrine of justification by faith (or through faith), in context of the first half of verse 4 it is probably an exhortation to wait patiently for the outcome, relying on one's faith to get one through. The prophet Habakkuk is urged to wait patiently and is assured that the justice will eventually be upheld.

Verses 6–20 contain five woe-oracles, focused on those who had done wicked deeds. Sometimes the oracle describes the nature of the evil deed. The punishment is designed to fit the particular evil deed (Anderson 2001, 226–27). The rhetorical intention is to convince the reader (and Habukkuk!) that those who commit injustice will be held accountable.

The fifth woe-oracle (vv. 18–20) is of particular interest to our study because of the reference to an idol which is mute. Verse 18 questions why anyone would make an idol. Though the maker trusts in the image, the idol is false and powerless. The idol is unable to speak. Verse 19 goes on to explain how the idol has no breath. The idol is not a living being. It is utterly ineffectual, in striking contrast to Yhwh, who is very powerful and who can speak to the human beings under care (Couey 2017, 254–55). According to Couey, "muteness is the most common disability assigned to idols in polemical texts. . . . It contrasts with Yhwh's ability to communicate with humans through various divinatory and revelatory channels, such as prophecy (cf. Isa 44:6–8)" (Couey 2017, 254). Yet, though one should urge the idol to communicate in some way, there will be no oracle from this image. Verse 20 ends the chapter by urging all to be silent before Yhwh, an ironic conclusion, to be sure.

Chapter 4 presents Yhwh as "super-able." Take verses 2 through 7, for example, where the deity's majesty fills the skies and splendor fills the earth. Pestilence and plague accompanied Yhwh. So powerful is Yhwh that the earth shook, the nations trembled, mountains shattered, and hills brought low. At the approach of the avenging deity, Habakkuk describes his physical reactions: "When I hear, and I tremble within; my lips quiver at the sound. Rottenness entered my bones, and my steps trembled under me. I wait quietly for the day of trouble to come upon the people who attack us" (v. 16). Yet, in verse 19, Habakkuk is strengthened by YHWH who makes his feet like the deer's and enables him to walk on the heights.

Of course, it is always useful to examine bodily metaphors in a study of disability in the Bible. In this case, the assumption that lack of speech would render someone unable to communicate is problematic. A person who is mute can use sign language or write a message. While many people would buy the idea that an idol would be unable to communicate, the assumption that muteness means the same thing in human beings is at issue here. Interestingly, like other biblical passages, those who await an attack from an enemy suffer fear, which is manifested physically. Also, the appearance of or presence of YHWH can cause a deep physical reaction.

Yet, perhaps most important is Habakkuk's focus on social justice. People with disabilities in the last sixty years or so, have organized to encourage justice within their own social settings. For those from Jewish and Christian traditions, Habakkuk can help serve as motivation for these justice pursuits.

ZEPHANIAH

The superscription to the book of Zephaniah (1:1) places the historical setting during the reign of "Josiah, son of Amon of Judah." Josiah's reign was ca. 640 to 621. After review of the evidence and careful consideration, Marvin A. Sweeney places Zephaniah's prophetic ministry during Josiah's reign, as he argues: "The specific concern with the purity of the temple as the holy center of creation and the use of sacrificial imagery on the Day of YHWH to purge the nation of idolatry indicate that the temple would be a likely setting for the prophet's speech, because of its central role in the religious life and theological perspective of the nation and because it is the most likely place to find people assembled for the public celebration of festivals" (Sweeney 2003, 16). He further suggests that Zephaniah spoke in support of King Josiah's reform agenda. Sweeney points out that Zephaniah is selective in his list of nations, namely: Philistia, Moab, Amon, Cush, and Assyria. These are nations with whom Judah was concerned in the era of Josiah's reign, rather than a postexilic context (Sweeney 2003, 17). Additionally, Israel and Judah had the experience of exile before the destruction of Jerusalem in 586 BCE, so references to exile do not necessarily point to post-exilic authorship of Zephaniah. In this section, Sweeney's placement of the book's composition is accepted here.

In verse 3 of chapter 1, YHWH intends to make the wicked stumble; this is a prophetic motif that indicates that stumbling will cause defeat. In other words, YHWH promises to defeat the wicked, to hold them accountable. Yet, the intention is also to cut off humanity from the face of the ground. Verses 4–6 focus on the deity's objective to destroy those who have been unfaithful to YHWH, whether to Baal, the host of heaven, or otherwise turned away from YHWH. Verse 7 suggests a priestly context where the deity plans a sacrificial feast and requires the people to purify themselves. Further on in chapter 1, the readers/listeners are reminded of the day of YHWH, a day which will be bleak and dark as wrong doers are held accountable. Verse 17 illustrates how dire things will be on the day of YHWH, should it come: "I will bring distress upon humanity. They shall walk like the blind, because they have sinned against YHWH. Their blood shall be poured out like dust and their flesh like refuse." The deity proposes to make the people walk as though they were visually impaired. Of course, we now know that people can be steady on their feet, in spite of any visual impairments. So, the presumption is that God would strike people with mobility issues.

At the beginning of chapter 2 of Zephaniah, the people are encouraged to pursue righteousness and humility before the day of YHWH. Perhaps in that case, a person may find shelter on that day. Verse 7 offers hope to the people, that after Ashkelon is deserted, the house of Judah may find sustenance there and their fortunes restored. As chapter 2 progresses, the enemies of Judah will be reduced and desolate, while the people of Judah may pillage the cities and villages to gain the articles were left behind. Interestingly, YHWH will purify the nations' speech as they gather on the day of YHWH. All people will call on the divine name and will serve YHWH "of one accord" (3:9). Zephaniah 3:13 states that the remnant of the Judean people will no longer do wrong nor will they utter lies; no longer would there be a "deceitful tongue" in their mouths. The metaphors of the mouth and tongue make tangible the former tendency toward dishonesty that now has been eradicated. The people who are honest will be able to lie down and rest without being troubled by others.

Later in Zephaniah 3:16 the people are encouraged to maintain hope and not let their hands droop (meaning do not let yourself give in to despair). The penultimate verse in the book, verse 19, reads: "Behold I will deal with all your oppressors at that time. I will save the limping one and I will gather the one who was driven out. I will turn their shame into praise and renown in all the earth." The "limping one" is used as example to illustrate how remarkably complete the restoration will be for the people of Judah. In an earlier essay, I commented on this passage and the equivalences made: "Of course, it is noteworthy that the lame person is paired with the outcast (v. 19). Perhaps this indicates some sort of social equivalence. Nevertheless, both characters are gathered in, and both experience renewal (יהריש, v. 17)" (Melcher 2007, 121).

HAGGAI

Most scholars are in agreement that Haggai prophesied in Judah between August 29 and December 18, 520 BCE. The book is very meticulous in dividing the discourse into five sections and precisely dating each one. As W. Eugene March points out, "Scholars basically accept these dates as authentic and believe the book was compiled in its present form only a short time after the prophet spoke, certainly before 515 BCE when the work on the Temple initiated at Haggai's urging was completed" (March 1996, 708–9). At this time, Judah was a sub-province of the Persian empire, known as *Yehud* rather than Judah. Darius I, the Great, the presiding King of Persia, was encouraging the restoration of *Yehud* and the rebuilding of the temple in Jerusalem. Darius continued the policies held by Cyrus, policies that avoided interference with the local governance and community practices as much as possible (Meyers and Meyers 1987, xxxii). Some of the valuable objects that were taken from the Jerusalem palace and temple by the Babylonians were returned to *Yehud* after the Persians conquered Babylon in 538.

As part of this tolerant policy toward local, indigenous leaders, Darius appointed Zerubbabel, grandson of King Jehoiachin, to be leader in *Yehud* (Meyers and Meyers 1987, xxxviii). Working in close co-leadership with Zerubbabel was the high priest Joshua, son of Jehozadak. Haggai and Zechariah strongly supported these appointees. As J. Maxwell Miller and John H. Hayes put it, "Associated with Zerubbabel in work on the temple was the priest Joshua (Jeshua), son of Jozadak" (Miller and Hayes 2006, 519). According to these scholars, unrest and conflict in the Persian empire from the death of Cambyses into the early years of Darius' reign "ignited prophetic fervor among the Jewish community and incited renewed efforts on temple reconstruction" (Miller and Hayes 2006, 520).

The focus of the two chapters is the Second Temple: the need to rebuild the temple, its legitimacy, and its authority. For the community—made up of returnees (from exile), of those who had remained in the land during exile, and of those who had migrated to Judah—the temple was the center of community life. Much of the book exhorts the community to undertake the rebuilding of the temple in earnest (for example, 1:5–11). Apparently, the community of *Yehud* had not prospered. The book of Haggai attributes this to the community's failure to rebuild the temple. The voice of YHWH tells the people that, if they rebuild the temple, then the agricultural return will be robust and the community will thrive.

At the end of chapter 1, verses 13–14, YHWH promises to be with Zerubbabel the governor and Joshua the high priest. Verse 14 reads, "Then YHWH roused the spirit of Zerubbabel son of Shealtiel, the governor of Judah, and the spirit of Joshua, son of Jehozadak, the high priest, and the spirit of all the remnant of the people. They came and worked on the house of YHWH of hosts, their God." This verse presumes that Haggai's prophecies are having the desired effect. Work on the Second Temple proceeds in earnest.

In Haggai 2:4–5 YHWH promises to be with the people and to have his spirit accompany them. Right on the heels of that promise, YHWH indicates the divine intention to "shake the heavens and the earth" and the nations as well (vv. 6–7), but then declares that valuable objects from the nations will come to the temple. However, later YHWH states that the work of the people and the people's offerings are defiled (v. 14) because they did not dedicate themselves to fulfilling YHWH's will. In verse 17 the deity reminds the listener/reader that they were struck with mildew, blight, and hail, and in all the works of their hands. In this instance, the text refers to agricultural diseases that afflict the plants (Petterson 2015, 78). However, they did not turn again to Yʜᴡʜ. The purpose of bringing these to the people was to encourage them to rededicate themselves to Yʜᴡʜ.

These verses from chapter 2 attribute ritual uncleanness to people because they have neglected cultic matters; that is, they have not rebuilt the temple. This is a possible explanation for the land's failure to thrive. It seems that everything that the people touch is defiled, made ritually unclean. The idea that those who are morally compromised would physically defile what they touch attributes ritual uncleanness to moral deficiency. Of course, for people with disabilities, both the association of moral wrongdoing and the attribution of physical defilement transmitted by touch is difficult to swallow.

ZECHARIAH

Many biblical scholars see a marked difference between two sections of Zechariah: chapters 1–8 and 9–14, known as First and Second Zechariah. These sections were likely produced from different authorship (Ollenburger 1996, 735).

First Zechariah consists of a set of eight visions, framed by two sermons (1:1–6 and 7:1–8:23). The chronological markers in chapters 1–8 place the approximate historical context during the reign of Darius I of Persia, in either his second year (520 BCE to early 519) or his fourth year (518) (Ollenburger 1996, 738). At this time, *Yehud* was likely to be a province in the Persian empire and existing under a tolerant policy designed to instill loyalty among subjects. Because of this policy, most of the important political and religious positions were held by locals (Ollenburger 1996, 738). More precisely, the appointed leaders of *Yehud* were generally returnees, those formerly in exile in Babylon.

According to Stephen L. Cook, the group responsible for Zechariah 1–8 was particularly focused on the central cult and temple (Cook 1995, 164–65). As he states, "The discussion above showed that the Zechariah group became more concerned with cult and temple as it underwent radicalization, culminating in the focus on cult and ritual in Zechariah 14. The group never lost its central-cult focus and was perhaps able to continue its activities within the temple throughout its history" (Cook 1995, 165).

Brian Peckham mentions that the return of the exiles caused conflict in Jerusalem. In Zechariah 8:16–17 and 18–19, the prophet appeals to the community to reach concord (Peckham 1993, 768).

Though the conflicts are more hinted at than referred to directly, the roots of the conflict likely lie in the disputes over property among those who had remained in the land and the exiles, who laid claim to ancestral property.

Zechariah tells of a future time when the nation will be restored and when the people will be safe from the hostilities by other nations. To illustrate divine protection, Yhwh promises to be a wall of fire around Jerusalem and a glory within it (2:5[9]). Of particular interest for this study is verse 8(12): "For thus says yhwh of hosts, 'After his glory sent me to the nations who plunder you: one who touches you touches the apple of my eye.'" As Ollenburger explains so well, "But here the imagery is uniquely physical; the exploitation of Judah or Zion, of God's people, is a poke in the pupil of God's eye" (Ollenburger 1996, 760). In response, those who plunder God's people will be plundered in turn by their former servants (v. 9[13]) as Yhwh waves the divine hand over them. According to Meyers and Meyers, "The entire verse . . . constitutes a divine pledge to Yehud that God is the instrument of her well-being" (Meyers and Meyers 1987, 167). The passage uses physical metaphors to convey the close, protective relationship between Yhwh and Yehud. It also expresses Yhwh's willingness to go to bat on behalf of God's people. Verses 14–15 reassure the community that yhwh will be with them, which is cause for rejoicing. Many nations will turn to Yhwh and commit to the divine. They, too, will become God's people.

Chapter 3 of Zechariah raises interesting issues of defilement for the priest Joshua. An angel instructs attendants to remove Joshua's filthy garments, then states, "I have removed your guilt and clothe you with rich robes" (v. 4). He was then clothed with a clean turban and priestly attire. The angel continues by giving Joshua an extended charge, duties not usually in the priests' domain (v. 7). He is assigned to the courts as well as to God's house. It is intriguing that Joshua's filthy garments are closely associated with guilt. When Joshua's dirty robes are removed, his guilt is lifted as well.

Zechariah 4:8–9 return to physical metaphors to describe Zerubbabel's powers and responsibilities. These verses indicate that Zerubbabel's hands started work on the temple and those hands will complete that work. The completion of the temple will make clear to the listener/reader that Yhwh sent Zechariah. These metaphors make the divine presence and intention palpable. It also establishes Zerubbabel as fulfilling God's intention for Yehud.

From the perspective of the past, Zechariah 7:8–14 persuades the reader that YHWH had emphasized the importance of justice to their ancestors. Justice is a topic which is always of significance when reading through a disability lens. In general, YHWH urged the community to render true justice and treat one another with loving kindness and compassion. The people were warned against defrauding the orphans, widows, strangers, and others. However, they refused to listen, turned a stubborn shoulder, and stopped their ears so that they will not hear (v. 11). They hardened their hearts against following the instructions given by the prophets, so God's wrath was kindled (v. 12).

Zechariah 8:16–17 reiterates concern for justice. These verses stress the importance of being honest with one another and executing justice in the gates. Also, the people are exhorted not to contrive evil or engage in perjury. The people are urged to love honesty and integrity.

Second Zechariah, chapters 9–14, is written in a strikingly different literary style from First Zechariah, chapters 1–8. In fact, some scholars have argued that Zechariah 9–11, 12–14, and Malachi are a "three-part prophetic collection, two parts of which are now joined artificially to Zechariah 1–8" (Ollenburger 1996, 740). There is little internal evidence tying these chapters 9–14 to Zechariah and scant hints pointing to a particular historical context generating these passages. The chapters envision a future time, as many prophetic books do, but they rely significantly on older Hebrew Bible passages. In a sense, these chapters re-envision the past to describe the future (Ollenburger 1996, 740). They also draw upon many literary forms to express their visions.

Zechariah 11 and 13 reflect a social context of conflict within the community. However, there is no way to date chapters 9–14 with any degree of certainty. According to Ollenburger,

> the commentary on chaps. 12–14 assumes that these materials are related to changes in Persian policy toward Judah and Jerusalem at the time of Nehemiah, just after the middle of the fifth century BCE. At this time, Persia sought to strengthen its control over, and military defenses within, the eastern Mediterranean area and

to more effectively centralize the administration of Judah in Jerusalem. Such social changes as these efforts brought about do not explain Second Zechariah, but they provide a plausible occasion for the violence and salvation that Jerusalem is expected to suffer, according to chaps. 12 and 14. (Ollenburger 1996, 742)

This study deems Ollenburger's observations about the historical context of Second Zechariah as credible and reasonable. The building of stronger military defenses in the mid-fifth century is supported by archeological discoveries on both sides of the Jordan River, in the coastal plain, and in the hill country (Meyers and Meyers 1993, 20). If the enhanced fortifications are dated to around 450 BCE, as is generally thought, they likely came about in response to the Greco-Persian wars of the previous decades and that continued into the mid-fifth century. In response to international instability affecting the provinces, with Egypt attempting to expand and stabilize their territories, Yehud would have been profoundly shaken. With tightened Persian controls over Yehud and the seeming hopelessness of the situation, the community of Yehud turned to eschatological understanding of history (Meyers and Meyers 1993, 21). Meyers and Meyers explain their position on the historical context of Zechariah:

> Some echoes of Israel's responses to these earthshaking events are surely preserved in the compendium of prophetic oracles we call Second Zechariah. . . . To be sure, Persia is nowhere explicitly mentioned in Zechariah 9–14. However, this situation can be understood as the function of the apocalyptic, or heightened eschatological, mode of the oracles. They move to the transhistorical realm precisely because of the apparently hopeless nature of the present reality. (Meyers and Meyers 1987, 21)

Second Zechariah divides clearly into two sections, chapters 9–11 and 12–14, based on content. Chapters 9–11 focus on the southern and northern tribal entities, Judah and Joseph. In chapters 12–14 the focus is more intra-community with discussion of the house of David, the people of Jerusalem, and the house of Judah (Boda 2016, 23). Mark J. Boda maintains that chapters 1–14 of Zechariah should be considered as a whole (Boda 2016, 27). First, both major sections, 1–8 and 9–14, make intertextual allusions to previous biblical passages. Both sections rely on Isaiah, Jeremiah, and Ezekiel with particular emphasis on Jeremiah. Prophetic sign-act forms are used in both major sections. Similar themes are developed across the sections. Boda maintains that there is a discernable editorial intention throughout the book (Boda 2016, 27–29).

Boda notes, however, that chapters 9–14 do not refer to the restoration of the community which suggests to him that the later historical context of the mid-fifth century may be the background for the section. Boda cites some evidence for his position on date: "The depiction of the march of a warrior from north to south in the Levant in 9:1–8, the mention of the Greeks in 9:13, and the focus on Egypt in chs. 10 and 14" (Boda 2016, 34). This helps to place the section in the time of Greek-Persian wars.

Of interest to our study is Zechariah 11:1–17, particularly the final verse. The pericope focuses on "worthless shepherds," leaders who failed the Judah community. Verse 17 states: "Woe to the worthless shepherd who abandons his flock. A sword shall be against his arm and the eye. His right arm will be completely withered and his right eye will be totally blinded." The worthless shepherd will be punished with a disabling condition. Note that this concerns the *right* arm. Most people are right-handed so this would significantly impair the individual.

Chapter 12, verse 3, contains a threat from Yhwh that Jerusalem shall become a heavy stone. All the peoples who attempt to lift it will injure themselves. Continuing in verse 4, the threat is to strike every horse with confusion and every rider with madness. Every horse of the peoples threatening Judah shall be stricken with blindness. Thus, the deity intends to physically harm any people who would attack Judah and this is the protection that the deity offers.

Unsurprisingly in a book that has an emphasis on the cult and proper worship, chapter 13, verse 1, states that a fountain will be provided where the house of David and the inhabitants of Jerusalem come to cleanse them of sin and iniquity. Once again, a physical remedy is promoted for moral failure.

Zechariah 14:12–15 depicts again how Yhwh will deal with the nations that waged war against Jerusalem. Their flesh, eyes, and tongues will rot away as they live. The wealth of the peoples fighting against Jerusalem will be plundered by the people of Judah. The plague will strike donkeys, mules, camels, and horses. In other words, the divine power over all things physical will be used to disable the nations who attack God's people.

MALACHI

Andrew E. Hill places the book of Malachi between the years 515 and 485 (or 480) BCE during the reign of the Persian King Darius I (Hill 1998, 51). The dates for the reign of Darius I are 521–486. Darius figures prominently in the postexilic biblical literature because the Second Temple was built during his reign. This historical background for the book of Malachi makes sense because the apocalyptic nature of the book presumes Yнwн's acting within history and the eventual success of the divine intention at a future time. Malachi reflects a clear-eyed observance of historical events on the part of the authorship. Hill suggests that the defeat of the Persian military by the Greeks at Marathon may have been a precipitating event for the composition of Malachi. "Such an event might easily be interpreted prophetically as a signal that Yahweh was about to 'shake the kingdoms of the earth' in accordance with Haggai's prior oracle (2:21–22). What better time to call the Hebrew restoration community to repentance?" (Hill 1998, 55).

Part of the background for understanding Malachi is the loss of confidence in Zerubbabel as orchestrating the restoration (Hill 1998, 75). This apparently led to some polarization in the community and the Levitical priesthood rose to prominence in Malachi's point of view. Clearly, the Yehud province was suffering severe economic deprivation. There is evidence of corruption among the officials, and some of them were making deals with the foreigners in the province (Neh 5:3, 7–8, 15; Hill 1998, 75).

The voice of Yнwн takes the priests to task for not giving enough respect in 1:6–8. The issue, according to these verses, is that the priests are violating protocol for making sacrifices in the temple. The voice of the deity accuses the priests of offering blind, lame, and sick animals on "the table of Yнwн." The passage suggests that a person would not offer such sacrifices to the governor and would not receive acceptance if these sacrifices had been offered (v. 8). Verse 9 raises the question of whether Yнwн would accept those who would offer sacrifices of such animals. This passage diminishes the value of any animal that has an impairment or illness. Unfortunately, it is not difficult to apply these parallel standards to human beings. The passage suggests that in God's eyes people with disabilities are disvalued as well.

Malachi 1:10–14 continues the theme condemning unsatisfactory sacrifices stating that this practice profanes the altar and expands the condemnation to those who would offer stolen animals. Verse 14 makes the strongest statement yet: "Cursed be the cheat who has a male in his flock, takes a vow, but sacrifices what is blemished to the Lord! For I am a great King—says YHWH of hosts—and my name will be revered among the nations."

Malachi 2:8–9 makes a direct claim against the Levitical priests stating that they did not follow the way of YHWH. In fact, the accusation is made that the priests made many people "stumble at the law" (v. 8). They have corrupted the covenant. In response, YHWH will make the priests contemptible and base in the sight of the people because the priests have shown partiality.

In chapter 3, verse 5, YHWH berates the people for not living up to covenant obligations of justice, particularly toward widows, and orphans, as well as oppressing the hired workers. This concern for justice on the part of the deity is reassuring.

Yet, later in chapter 3 the deity promises restoration, saying that if the people return to YHWH, then YHWH will turn again to them. For those who revere YHWH's name, "the sun of righteousness shall rise with healing in her wings" (3:20; 4:2 in some English versions). What the nature of that healing might be is unclear, though subsequent verses indicate that sons and fathers will again turn their hearts toward one another.

THEOLOGICAL IMPLICATIONS

The theme of "stumbling" occurs among the Twelve as it has in the larger prophetic books. It signifies failure on the part of the nation, particularly the failure to follow a righteous path, one that includes adherence to YHWH's covenant stipulations. The motif of stumbling tends to shape in the reader a proclivity to attribute stumbling to unrighteous behavior. With this mindset inculcated by the motif of stumbling, the reader tends to attribute wrongdoing to those who are unsteady on their feet. When interpreting these passages, one should challenge this tendency explicitly.

We have seen in this chapter of the study that YHWH has the power to heal, but sometimes refuses to do so because of the people's sinfulness. This concept is especially odious to people with disabilities who have been prayed over repeatedly with the expectation that God would heal or cure the individual with a disability. When healing does not happen, passages like these in the Book of the Twelve might lead the reader to assume that healing does not occur in the here and now because of sinfulness. Interpreters should challenge this representation in the biblical text.

In Hosea 9:11–17 the focus is on infertility and premature death for children. Many scholars have argued that infertility was considered a disability in ancient Israel and Judah. This passage from Hosea presents infertility as a consequence of sinful behavior, a punishment coming from Yhwh. While in a modern context, infertility may not be considered a disability, to view the deity as inflicting this punishment is disturbing. In this interpreter's opinion, it is better to perceive infertility as a random occurrence, rather than inflicted by God. The death of innocent children is also portrayed in this section of Hosea 9.

Particularly helpful in the Book of the Twelve, from a theological point of view, is the emphasis on socioeconomic disparities among the people of Israel. Amos is a good example of this emphasis. As mentioned above, many people with disabilities have lived in poverty. Amos takes those to task who have oppressed or taken advantage of the poor. Anyone who has gained wealth by oppressing the poor is subjected to God's punishment.

An interesting irony arises because Yhwh promises to help Judah by protecting the people against the nations who would attack them. This is ironic because in other cases Yhwh is the one who inflicts damage upon Judah or Yehud. However, there are passages in the Twelve that allude to Yhwh's compassion or sympathy for Israel. This is a positive representation of the deity, one who feels sadness for those who go through pain.

Another issue that arises among the Twelve is the association of defilement with disability. Malachi focuses concerns with uncleanness or impurity on the sacrifices that are offered in the sanctuary. Yhwh criticizes the priests for not offering pure, unblemished animals in the temple. The deity makes it clear that such animals are not appropriate for offerings to God. It implies that people with disabilities are not appropriate to approach the altar in worship. We certainly want to challenge such a viewpoint.

Conclusion

Prophetic Disability and Theological Ethics

One issue raised early in the book of Isaiah and repeated in other prophets is the use of the metaphor of the wounded body to connote unfaithfulness. Disobedience to Yhwh is manifested in the prophetic literature often as a wounded body, such as in Isaiah 1, for example. There the body is depicted as covered with bruises, sores, and bleeding wounds as from repeated beatings. The people have been rebellious, according to the deity's speech in this chapter. One of Nussbaum's values for quality of life is to have bodily integrity, to be free of assault from others (Nussbaum 2006, 76). In this case, God is depicted as the source of bodily assault. Some people alive today have developed disabilities as a result of assault and to depict the deity in such a way is to create distance and make God difficult to approach. This portrayal of Yhwh as abuser could be a trigger for the person whose experience of assault resulted in their having a disability.

A recurring theme in the prophets arises in language of stumbling or falling (Jer 13:16; 20:10–11; 46:6, 12, etc.). Many occasions in the ongoing exegesis of these prophetic books we have encountered the themes of stumbling or falling. Often falling represents military defeat or the failure of Judah/Yehud to defend themselves. Stumbling can also connote an inability to stay on the path of righteousness, to follow in Yhwh's ways. As noted above, this can form an association between difficulties with mobility/unsteadiness and rebelliousness/sinfulness. Such attributions have plagued people with disabilities for hundreds of years. It is very important to counter such attributions with the idea that people with disabilities are no more or less righteous than others.

Another repeated metaphor is the inability of people to follow Yhwh's paths or a deliberate turning from the way (see Isa 30:11, 20–21; Jer 14:10; 23:12, etc.). The end of Isaiah, chapter 35, envisions all God's people being able to follow the path. The redeemed and the ransomed will return to the land by means of this path (vv. 9–10). This is an inclusive vision where all who follow Yhwh will be able to stay on the broad path and return to their homeland. Of course, earlier verses presume Yhwh's healing of people with disabilities so that the broad path home will be easier to follow (see, especially, vv. 5 and 6).

A major issue that arises from many of the biblical passages we have studied; that Yhwh causes disability or illness through divine means, such as seen in Isaiah 6:10 (see above). This is present also in Ezekiel 5:12–17 where people shall die of pestilence or famine, by the sword, and they will be mocked by the surrounding nations. Prophetic passages often depict Yhwh as determining who shall be injured or ill, who shall be weakened or strengthened. The sovereignty of God entails divine power over bodies and their appropriate functioning. Often the determination between leaving the human healthy and inflicting injury or illness has to do with whether the person is deserving of punishment. Yhwh tends to decide whether or not to inflict punishment based on whether the human being has committed sin/transgression. Yet, if the person has been punished sufficiently, then Yhwh may suspend further discipline of the subject. Often, at some point, Yhwh will turn to forgiveness and restoration, rather than continue to exact punishment.

Though often there is movement toward restoration and forgiveness on the part of the deity, yet the primary concern remains. These passages present God as having complete discretion to decide on whether a person remains healthy or whether they will experience some kind of impairment. The nature of the illness or injury does not matter; God still has complete power and discretion to impact human bodies in whatever manner. Fertility and childbirth are cases in point. Yhwh is presented as having control over women's wombs and exerting that control in certain situations. The deity can and will stop fertility as part of a punishment. This tendency can be generalized to other bodily functions as well. The sovereignty of God extends to human bodies. Sometimes this sovereignty manifests as divine providence, as protection over human bodies. At times it manifests differently, as authoritative control and jurisdiction over human health and well-being.

To picture the deity as doling out health or illness based on a person's righteousness has some troublesome theological and ethical implications. In fact, this works in contrast to Nussbaum's values for quality of life—for example, for a human being to have a long life and to have good health, including reproductive health (Nussbaum 2006, 76). While it is true that the people of Judah have feet of clay, yet they also have a right to good quality of life. As the prophets present YHWH, the deity's actions are sometimes in conflict with the ethics inherent in Nussbaum's quality of life values. To present the deity as taking action that conflicts with the well-being of the people of God can discourage people from seeking a closer relationship with God.

On the other hand, there can be issues with God's healing (Isa 33:24); issues with curing (Isa 35:5–6). While the prophets present YHWH as having the power and sometimes the inclination to heal people of their illnesses, injuries, or disabilities, not everyone is healed. The depiction of God as healer does raise the question of why many are not healed. What are the reasons for some being excluded from healing? If a person is not healed, perhaps one could attribute sinfulness to that person. Also, sometimes a person's disability is integral to their identity. Some feel that if the disability were removed, then they would not recognize themselves. In addition, sometimes it seems that healing for those with disabilities is linked to an intention to remove such persons from view, to make people with disabilities disappear.

There are instances where superhuman strength is assigned to different characters in the prophetic texts, in the ideal king (Isa 11) and in the Assyrians (Isa 5:26–30). God is also portrayed as super-powerful and wrathful (Isa 30:27–33). In Isaiah 41 the Israelites are portrayed as powerful warriors, with God's help. Though the purpose of depicting some people as superpowerful is intended to warn the people of the harm that could come to them from the nations, it is also intended to instill fear in the reader/listener. The depictions are unrealistic and they enhance the distance between those without disabilities and those with disabilities.

Another contrast between God's power and sovereignty and humanity's impermanence and fragility is made in Isaiah 40 as well as in other passages. At times people with disabilities seem to serve as a foil to demonstrate the awesomeness of God.

Some of the passages represent God as helping the former exiles to return to their homeland. The assumption of these texts is that people with disabilities need God's help to get back to the land. The writers assume that people with disabilities cannot get back on their own nor with help from family and friends.

The suffering servant is portrayed as carrying the sins of others and suffering for the sake of Israel. If we accept the theory that the suffering servant is a representation of a person with a disability, it is offensive to indicate that the purpose of the suffering is to help the nation's people. What about the inherent need of people with disabilities to reduce suffering for their own sake, not for the sake of others?

In some ways, it appears that being female was a disability in ancient Israel and Judah. Carole Fontaine has suggested that this is reflected in biblical passages. From what we have seen, this is a good theory. There are parallels between how women and people with disabilities are treated. This arises periodically throughout this study.

The passages in the prophets allude to strong pressure to adhere to the divine will. Did people really have a choice? Look at the divine tactics to enforce obedience. There was much pressure from the deity such as threats of physical punishment or death. While the goal was to get the people to return to God, still, threats of physical punishment, war, and destruction of the land are very dire tactics. These tactics do not enhance the sense of people returning to God out of their free choice.

Of course, idols are represented as disabled. Many passages construct a notable contrast between God's ability and idols' disabilities. To demonstrate idols' ineffectual nature as compared to Yhwh, the idols are represented as unable to speak or hear and unable to respond favorably to requests. This is an unfavorable representation for people with disabilities. While all people have limitations, that does not mean that they are ineffectual. Perhaps their gifts lie in unexpected areas.

The exhortation to do justice and be righteous occurs in numerous passages in the prophetic corpus; for example, in Jeremiah 7 and 22. These texts about justice are among the most promising passages in the prophets for people with disabilities. There is a concern for the marginalized in prophetic appeals to act justly. Though the biblical passages about justice often refer to the widow, the orphan, or the foreigner, these are representative categories and do not constitute an exhaustive list. A concern for people with disabilities recognizes that they are sometimes treated as marginalized. Justice is attentive to inequities and discrimination. Justice is also attentive to people who are at risk in the community.

Related to issues of justice is the concern for the poor. The book of Amos especially demonstrates a concern for the poor. The demographics of poverty make clear that many among the disabled are living in poverty. Amos can serve as an inspiration for those seeking to help people with disabilities to escape poverty. This prophetic book critiques those people who would take advantage of or oppress the poor. The book criticizes the wealthy for being inattentive to the plight of the poor and for exacerbating income disparities.

The present study has explored many pertinent passages in the prophets to explore the nature of metaphors about disability. There may be themes or motifs that I have missed, but this has furthered our understanding of passages treating disability, especially as they relate to divine sovereignty. The multifaceted approach to the exploration of individual passages, using insights from historical, social, and cultural backgrounds, has enabled us to see more fully the treatment of persons with disabilities in the prophetic literature.

Bibliography

Anderson, Francis I. 2001. *Habakkuk: A New Translation with Commentary*. AB 25. New Haven: Yale University Press.

Balzer, Klaus. 2001. *Deutero-Isaiah: A Commentary on Isaiah 40–55*. Minneapolis: Fortress.

Baumgartner, Walter, and Ludwig Koehler. 2001. *The Hebrew and Aramaic Lexicon of the Old Testament*. Vol. 1. Leiden: Brill.

Bhaskar, Roy, and Berth Danermark. 2006. "Metatheory, Interdisciplinarity and Disability Research: A Critical Realist Perspective." *Scandinavian Journal of Disability Research* 8, no. 4: 278–97.

Blenkinsopp, Joseph. 2000. *Isaiah 1–39: A New Translation with Introduction and Commentary*. AB 19. New York: Doubleday.

———. 2000. *Isaiah 40–55: A New Translation with Introduction and Commentary*. AB 19A. New York: Doubleday.

———. 2003. *Isaiah 56–66: A New Translation with Introduction and Commentary*. AB 19B. New York: Doubleday.

Block, Daniel I. 1997. *The Book of Ezekiel: Chapters 1–24*. NICOT. Grand Rapids: Eerdmans.

———. 1998. *The Book of Ezekiel: Chapters 25–48*. NICOT. Grand Rapids: Eerdmans.

———. 2013. *By the River Chebar: Historical, Literary, and Theological Studies in the Book of Ezekiel*. Eugene, Ore.: Cascade, 2013. Boadt, Lawrence, C. S. P. 1997. "The Poetry of Prophetic Persuasion: Preserving the Prophet's Persona." *CBQ* 59: 1–21.

Boda, Mark J. 2016. *Zechariah*. NICOT. Grand Rapids: Eerdmans.

Carroll R., M. Daniel. 2020. *The Book of Amos*. NICOT. Grand Rapids: Eerdmans.

Carroll, Robert P. 2004. *Jeremiah*. London: T&T Clark.

Christiensen, Duane L. 2009. *Nahum: A New Translation and Commentary*. AB 24F. New York: Yale University Press.

Claassens, L. Juliana. 2014. "The Rhetorical Function of the Woman in Labor Metaphor in Jeremiah 30–31." *Journal of Theology for Southern Africa* 250: 67–84.

Cogan, Mordechai. 1999. "Chapter Seven: Into Exile: From the Assyrian Conquest of Israel to the Fall of Babylon." Pages 242–75 in *The Oxford History of the Biblical World*. Edited by Michael D. Coogan. Oxford: Oxford University Press.

Coogan, Michael D. 2014. *The Old Testament: A Historical and Literary Introduction to the Hebrew Scriptures*. 3rd ed. Oxford: Oxford University Press.

Cook, Stephen L. 1995. *Prophecy & Apocalypticism: The Postexilic Social Setting*. Minneapolis: Fortress.

Couey, J. Blake. 2017. "Isaiah, Jeremiah, Ezekiel, Daniel, and the Twelve." Pages 215–73 in *The Bible and Disability: A Commentary*. Edited by Sarah J. Melcher, Micheal C. Parsons, and Amos Yong. SRTD. Waco, Tex.: Baylor University Press.

———. 2015. *Reading the Poetry of First Isaiah: The Most Perfect Model of the Prophetic Poetry*. Oxford: Oxford University Press.

Creamer, Deborah Beth. 2009. *Disability and Christian Theology: Embodied Limits and Constructive Possibilities*. Oxford: Oxford University Press.

Crouch, Carly L. 2020. "Playing Favourites: Israel and Judah in the Metaphor of Marriage in Jeremiah 3." *JSOT* 44, no. 4: 594–609.

Cuéllar, Gregory L. 2015. "J. Severino Croatto's Rereading of Empire in Isaiah 47." *BibInt* 23: 222–47.

Darr, Katheryn Pfisterer. 1994. "The Book of Ezekiel: Introduction, Commentary, and Reflections." Pages 1073–607 in *The New Interpreter's Bible*, vol. 6. Nashville: Abingdon.

Dearman, J. Andrew. 2010. *The Book of Hosea*. NICOT. Grand Rapids: Eerdmans.

Duhm, Bernard. 1922. *Das Buch Jesaja*. 4th ed. Gottingen: S. Hirzel.

Ellis, Teresa Ann. 2009. "Jeremiah 44: What If the 'Queen of Heaven' Is YHWH?" *JSOT* 33, no. 4: 465–88.

Fontaine, Carole R. 2007. "'Be Men, O Philistines' (1 Samuel 4:9): Iconographic Representations and Reflections on Female Gender as Disability in the Ancient World." Pages 61–72 in *This Abled Body: Rethinking*

Disabilities in Biblical Studies. Edited by Hector Avalos, Sarah J. Melcher, and Jeremy Schipper. Atlanta: SBL.

Franzmann, Majella. 1995. "The City as Woman: The Case of Babylon in Isaiah 47." *Australian Biblical Review* 43: 1–20.

Freedy, Karl S., and Redford, Donald B. 1970. "The Dates of Ezekiel in Relation to Biblical, Babylonian, and Egyptian Sources." *JAOS* 90: 462–85.

Frymer-Kensky, Tikva. 1992. *In the Wake of the Goddesses: Women, Culture, and the Biblical Transformation of Pagan Myth*. New York: The Free Press.

Gaventa, William C., and David L. Coulter, eds. 2003. *The Pastoral Voice of Robert Perske*. New York: Haworth Pastoral.

Goldingay, John. 1998. "Isaiah I 1 and II 1." *VT* 48, no. 3: 326–32.

Harding, James E. 2015. "The Silent Goddess and the Gendering of Divine Speech in Jeremiah 44." Pages 208–23 in *Jeremiah in Feminist and Postcolonial Perspective*. Edited by Christi M. Maier and Carolyn J. Sharp. London: Bloomsbury T&T Clark.

Harger, Adam K. 2019. "Reading Jeremiah 52 in Exile: Purpose in the Composition of Jeremiah." *JTS* 70, no. 2: 511–22.

Hiebert, Theodore. 1996. "The Book of Habakkuk: Introduction, Commentary, and Reflections." Pages 623–55 in *The New Interpreter's Bible*, vol. 7. Nashville: Abingdon.

Hill, Andrew E. 1998. *Malachi: A New Translation and Commentary*. AB 25D. New York: Doubleday.

Holladay, William L. 1986. *Jeremiah 1: A Commentary on the Book of the Prophet Jeremiah Chapters 1–25*. Philadelphia: Fortress.

———. 1989. *Jeremiah 2: A Commentary on the Book of the Prophet Jeremiah Chapters 26–52*. Minneapolis: Fortress.

Kalmanofsky, Amy. 2008. "Israel's Baby: The Horror of Childbirth in the Biblical Prophets." *BibInt* 16: 60–82.

———. 2011. "The Dangerous Sisters of Jeremiah and Ezekiel." *JBL* 130, no. 2: 299–312.

Kelle, Brad E. 2010. "Hosea 4–14 in Twentieth-Century Scholarship." *CurBR* 8, no. 3: 314–75.

Kessler, Rainer. 2008. *The Social History of Ancient Israel: An Introduction*. Translated by Linda M. Mahoney. Minneapolis: Fortress.

Kidner, Derek. 2014. *Jeremiah*. Downers Grove, Ill.: IVP Academic.

Klein, Ralph W. 1988. *Ezekiel: The Prophet and His Message*. Studies on Personalities of the Old Testament. Columbia: University of South Carolina Press.

Lundbom, Jack R., ed. 2004. *Jeremiah 37–52*. New York: Doubleday.

Makujina, John. 2016. "Male Obstetric Competence in Ancient Israel: A Response to Two Recent Proposals." *VT* 66, no. 1: 78–94.

March, W. Eugene. 1996. "The Book of Haggai: Introduction, Commentary, and Reflections." Pages 705–32 in *The New Interpreter's Bible*, vol. 7. Nashville: Abingdon.

Mays, James Luther. 1969. *Hosea: A Commentary*. Philadelphia: Westminster.

———. 1976. *Micah: A Commentary*. Philadelphia: Westminster.

Melcher, Sarah J. 2011. "A Tale of Two Eunuchs: Isaiah 56:1–8 and Acts 8:26–40." Pages 117–28 in *Disability Studies and Biblical Literature*. Edited by Candida R. Moss and Jeremy Schipper. New York: Palgrave Macmillan.

———. 2017. "Genesis and Exodus." Pages 29–56 in *The Bible and Disability: A Commentary*. Edited by Sarah J. Melcher, Mikeal C. Parsons, and Amos Yong. SRTD. Waco, Tex.: Baylor University Press.

———. 2007. "With Whom Do the Disabled Associate? Metaphorical Interplay in the Latter Prophets." Pages 115–29 in *This Abled Body: Rethinking Disabilities in Biblical Studies*. Edited by Hector Avalos, Sarah J. Melcher, and Jeremy Schipper. Atlanta: SBL.

Meldon, Perri. N.d. *Disability History: Military and Disability (U.S. National Park Service)*. Accessed August 15, 2020. https://www.nps.gov/articles/disabilityhistorymilitary.htm.

Melugin, Roy F., and Marvin A. Sweeney, eds. 1996. *New Visions of Isaiah*. JSOTSupp 214. Sheffield, England: Sheffield Academic Press.

Meyers, Carol L., and Eric M. Meyers. 1987. *Haggai and Zechariah 1–8: A New Translation, Introduction, and Commentary*. AB 25B. Garden City, N.Y.: Doubleday.

———. 1993. *Zechariah 9–14: A New Translation with Introduction and Commentary*. AB 25C. New York: Doubleday.

Miller, J. Maxwell, and John H. Hayes. 2006. *A History of Ancient Israel and Judah*. 2nd ed. Louisville: Westminster John Knox.

National Council on Disability. 2017. "Highlighting Disability / Poverty Connection, NCD Urges Congress to Alter Federal Policies that Disadvantage People with Disabilities." https://ncd.gov/newsroom/2017/disability-poverty-connection-2017-progress-report-release. Accessed March 12, 2022.

Niditch, Susan. 1980. "The Composition of Isaiah 1." *Bib* 61, no. 4: 509–29.

Nussbaum, Martha C. 2006. *Frontiers of Justice: Disability, Nationality, Species Membership*. Cambridge, Mass.: Harvard University Press.

O'Connor, Kathleen M. 2011. *Jeremiah: Pain and Promise*. Minneapolis: Fortress.

Odell, Margaret S. 2005. *Ezekiel*. Smyth & Helwys Bible Commentary. Macon, Ga.: Smyth and Helwys.

Ollenburger, Ben C. 1996. "The Book of Zechariah: Introduction, Commentary, and Reflections." Pages 733–840 in *The New Interpreter's Bible*, vol. 7. Nashville: Abingdon.

Olyan, Saul M. 2008. *Disability in the Hebrew Bible: Interpreting Mental and Physical Differences*. Cambridge: Cambridge University Press.

Paul, Shalom M. 2012. *Isaiah 40–66: Translation and Commentary*. Grand Rapids: Eerdmans.

Peckham, Brian. 1993. *History and Prophecy: The Development of Late Judean Literary Traditions*. New York: Doubleday.

Petterson, Anthony R. 2015. *Haggai, Zechariah, and Malachi*. Apollos Old Testament Commentary 25. Downers Grove, Ill.: IVP.

Raphael, Rebecca. 2008. *Biblical Corpora: Representations of Disability in Hebrew Biblical Literature*. New York: T&T Clark.

———. 2011. "Whoring after Cripples: On the Intersection of Gender and Disability in Jeremiah." Pages 103–16 in *Disability and Biblical Literature*. Edited by Candida R. Moss and Jeremy Schipper. New York: Palgrave Macmillan.

Reinders, Hans S. 2014. *Disability, Providence, and Ethics: Bridging Gaps, Transforming Lives*. SRTD. Waco, Tex.: Baylor University Press.

Rendtorff, Rolf. 1996. "The Book of Isaiah: A Complex Unity: Synchronic and Diachronic Reading." Pages 32–49 in *New Visions of Isaiah*. Edited by Roy F. Melugin and Marvin A. Sweeney. Sheffield: Sheffield Academic.

Roberts, J. J. M. 2015. *First Isaiah: A Commentary*. Minneapolis: Fortress.

Routledge, Robin. 2020. *Hosea: A Commentary*. Tyndale Old Testament Commentaries 24. Downers Grove, Ill.: IVP.

Sanders, James. 1997. "The Exile and Canon Formation." Pages 37–61 in *Exile: Old Testament, Jewish, and Christian Conceptions*. Edited by James M. Scott. JSJSup. Leiden: Brill.

Schipper, Jeremy. 2011. *Disability and Isaiah's Suffering Servant*. Oxford: Oxford University Press.

———. 2015. "Why Does Imagery of Disability Include Healing in Isaiah?" *JSOT* 39, no. 3: 219–33.

Sen, Amartya. 1992. *Inequality Reexamined*. Oxford: Clarendon.

Shakespeare, Tom. 2014. *Disability Rights and Wrongs Revisited*. 2nd ed. London: Routledge.

Simundson, Daniel J. 1996. "The Book of Micah: Introduction, Commentary, and Reflections." Pages 533–89 in *The New Interpreter's Bible*, vol. 7. Nashville: Abingdon.

Smith-Christopher, D. L. 1997. "Reassessing the Historical and Sociological Impact of the Babylonian Exile (597/587–539 BCE)." Pages 7–36 in *Exile: Old Testament, Jewish, and Christian Conceptions*. Edited by James M. Scott. JSJSup. Leiden: Brill.

Smith-Christopher, Daniel L. 2015. *Micah: A Commentary*. OTL. Philadelphia: Westminster John Knox.

Staples, Jason A. 2021. *The Idea of Israel in Second Temple Judaism: A New Theory of People, Exile, and Israelite Identity*. Cambridge: Cambridge University Press.

Stulac, Daniel J. 2018. *History and Hope: The Agrarian Wisdom of Isaiah 28–35*. University Park, Pa.: Eisenbrauns.

Sweeney, Marvin A. 2003. *Zephaniah: A Commentary*. Hermeneia. Minneapolis: Fortress.

———. 2016. *Isaiah 40–66*. Grand Rapids: Eerdmans.

Watson, Nick. 2012. "Researching Disablement." Pages 93–106 in *Routledge Handbook of Disability Studies*. Edited by Nick Watson, Alan Roulstone, and Carol Thomas. New York: Routledge.

Williams, Simon J. 1999. "Is Anybody There? Critical Realism, Chronic Illness, and the Disability Debate." *Sociology of Health and Illness* 21, no. 6: 797–819.

Wolff, Hans Walter. 1974. *Hosea: A Commentary on the Book of the Prophet Hosea*. Translated by Gary Stansell. Hermeneia. Minneapolis: Augsburg.

Yong, Amos. 2007. *Theology and Down Syndrome: Reimagining Disability in Late Modernity*. SRTD. Waco, Tex.: Baylor University Press.

Zimmerli, Walther. 1979. *Ezekiel 1: A Commentary on the Book of the Prophet Ezekiel, Chapters 1–24*. Translated by Ronald F. Clements. Hermeneia. Philadelphia: Fortress.

———. 1983. *Ezekiel 2: A Commentary on the Book of the Prophet Ezekiel, Chapters 25–48*. Translated by James D. Martin. Hermeneia. Philadelphia: Fortress.

Index of Names

Index of Subjects

ability-based metaphors, 25
Ahaz, 12, 18
Amorites, 86
Amos (book of), 109; dating, 84–85; social justice concerns in, 85–86, 103
Amos (prophet), 84
animal metaphors, 12–13
Aram, 85
Aristotelian ethics, 6
arrogance, 15–16, 40
Assyria, 81–83; and arrogance, 17; Babylonian defeat of, 90; and the book of Amos, 84–85; defeat of, 89–90; destruction of, 23; and God's sovereignty, 19; military forces of, 16, 41–42; as punishment for Judah, 17, 41

Babylon: conquest of Judah, 52–53, 57–58; exiles in, 32, 58–59, 63, 66, 70–72, 74–75; fighting Egypt, 56–57, 69–70, 90; God punishing, 52; King of, 31, 58; oppression by,

32; as punishment for Judah, 41; as Queen, 31–32; and Sidon, 69
Babylonians, 19–20, 26
beatings, 13, 37, 105
Biblical Corpora (Raphael), 7
blindness, 20–21, 29; cure for, 21–22, 41, 59; and humility, 22; as metaphor, 29–31, 47, 67, 76; not promised healing, 30, 59; and returning exiles, 54
bodily metaphors, 15–16, 21, 92; *see also* physical metaphors; wounded body metaphors
body imagery, 18–19

cake metaphor, 82
Chaldean invasion, 90
childbirth metaphor, 84; *see also* women
children/infants, God threatening to kill, 83–84, 89–90, 103
circumcision, 48
cleanliness, 14, 16
cleansing, 17, 38, 75, 77, 100

119

Index of Scripture